"Your real clock is inside your chest—called your heart. So you don't have a second to lose in pursuing the quality of life you desire. For when the clock stops, it's all over!"

Inspired by
The Meaning of Life
Bradley Trevor Greive

WARREN "TRAPPER" WOODS, CSP
WILLIAM A. GUILLORY, Ph.D.

Tick Tock! Who Broke the Clock?
Copyright © by Warren Woods, CSP
and
William A. Guillory, Ph.D.

First Edition: 2003
LCCN: 2003101281
ISBN: 0-933241-18-6
Printed in the United States of America

Cover design by Kent Hansen

Published by
Innovations International, Inc.,
Publishing Division
310 East 4500 South, Suite 420
Salt Lake City, Utah, 84107
innovationsintl@qwest.net

This book is dedicated to those who influence most our quality of life — Brenda and Katie

Acknowledgments

The authors would like to acknowledge the effort and dedication of Deborah McClelland, especially in the early stages when the book was just taking form. Her contribution was invaluable. We are also grateful for those who have served to continually teach us the lessons of life that have significantly influenced our choices and the material for this book. They are far too many to list here by name. Finally, we are thankful to those who are responsible for the design and accuracy of the text – Tatiana Clark and our editor, Becky Harding.

The Seven Steps to Better Work-Life Balance

1. Understand the new time paradigm – work and personal activities are inseparable.

2. Take a personal inventory of your life – to determine the gaps.

3. Adopt a mind-set of 100% responsibility and 100% accountability – for the state of your life.

4. Rewrite the script of your life – based upon your innermost values.

5. Resolve your greatest barrier to achieving work-life quality – in spite of the consequences.

6. Learn to better manage your life – by practicing self-management skills.

7. Live the new script of your life – and acquire the balance and quality you deserve!

Tick Tock Who Broke the Clock?
Solving the Work-Life Balance Equation

Table of Contents

Foreword

This book is written for every individual who dreams of living a more satisfying and meaningful life. It is the cooperative effort and expertise of Warren "Trapper" Woods, CSP and William A. Guillory, Ph.D. Each brings vast understanding and foresight to the dilemma of work-life quality and balance. This work includes many of their personal, individual, and shared experiences. For continuity throughout the book, the information is presented in the first person without distinguishing who is actually speaking.

A decade ago, our career decisions included technical competencies and management skills that offered the shortest and most direct route to big salaries and important sounding titles. Today, our biggest priority is balance and a quality life. We are even willing to sacrifice a little money and prestigious positions to create rewarding lives for ourselves that integrate purposeful work, meaningful relationships, and gratifying experiences.

The depth of a person's desire for a richer, more fulfilling life experience will determine how she or he proceeds through the following pages. Since this is written for you and not the collective we and us or the infamous *they*, I am now going to stop being ambiguous and direct my remarks to you as if you and I were conversing together one-on-one. You can read this book merely for information or you can dive in headfirst and allow yourself to experience and embrace the principles herein, which will endow you with the power to transform your world.

The basic premise of this manuscript is this: *Your work and your personal life are inseparable.* You have, more likely than not, felt the effect of that certainty in the form of frustration over needing to do a little work from home and feeling the guilt of taking time away from your family or perhaps the disappointment, even resentment, of being unable to attend your daughter's soccer game (or some other personal event that was important to you) in the middle of a busy workday.

This book is about *integrating* your work and personal life. You will find principles and guidelines that will help you organize your life in this new way of thinking instead of society's rewards system. Unlike amusement park rides where you are instructed to keep your arms and hands inside at all times and to remain seated until the ride comes to a complete stop, I encourage you to jump into this adventure with reckless abandon and risk discovering just how congruent you are with yourself and, more specifically, what's really important to you.

- In *chapter one* you will gain a better understanding of the new *integrated* time paradigm.

- *Chapter two* gives you the tools to help you take a thorough personal inventory of the state of your life to determine the gaps between how your life is and how you would like it to be.

- *Chapter three* suggests you adopt a mind-set of 100% responsibility and 100% accountability for the state of your life; a challenging but empowering state of mind.

- *Chapter four* will help you rewrite the script of your life based upon your innermost values.

- In *chapter five* you will learn life-quality skills that will help you live your script on a daily basis.

- In *chapter six* you will learn how to *choose* those activities that yield the highest life quality return on your investment and how to *avoid* those that have little or no return.

- In *chapter seven* you will learn tools for life-management.

- And finally, in the *afterword,* you will be encouraged to consciously create your legacy by the way you live your life.

When you have completed this personal journey you will perhaps come to the realization, as did I, that you cannot manage time, you can only manage yourself. More than anything, I hope you feel empowered and excited with your new understanding of how to integrate your living (self), your earning (work), your loved ones (family), and your serving (service).

I hope your experience within these pages translates into more contentment, more excitement, more happiness, more passion, more quality, more balance, and consequently more satisfaction in your life.

One more thing, **please write in this book**! Without writing the exercises you will receive considerably less value. Keep in mind, there will be many other copies available to buy for friends and family.

I encourage you to fully experience and enjoy the ride.

Introduction

As I awaited the birth of my first daughter, time appeared to plod along at such a slow pace, I wondered if I could move it along faster by counting the ticks of the clock, or mentally inducing my wife's labor. On the other hand, when I vacationed at a Monterey condominium on the Pacific Ocean, time appeared to move so fast that I found myself desperately holding on to each pleasurable moment. In truth, time is neither fast nor slow.

Time, as we define it, is constant and moves progressively from the past, through the present, to the future. Time is steady. It does not slow down even when we are bored or anxious. By the same token, time does not speed up, but it certainly feels like it does when we are excited and fully experiencing an event. The truth is, we *experience* events in our lives at different rates.

I have come to the conclusion that time does not exist! What exists are events that I can choose to experience in a variety of ways. Time takes care of itself.

What I really need, in order to experience life in a way that is genuinely satisfying, is a basis for choosing the events that I want to experience. My first impulse is to make my decisions using the values defined by my parents, my religion, my community, my society, my culture, my friends ... and on and on it goes without me asking myself, "What's really important to *me*?"

It's a simple question. "What's really important to *me*?" The answer, however, can be both scary and dangerous. Scary in the sense that it's a little like putting your quarter in the slot machine and pulling the lever, or clicking "send" on an email you can't recall, or sliding down a smooth chute with nothing to grab on to.

Dangerous because you may discover you have values and ideas that are contrary to the very foundations you've built your life on. Maybe you'll come to the conclusion you were born into the wrong family because you have so very little in common with them. You've always wondered why they insist on gathering every weekend to eat, drink, and argue insistently about subjects you have little or no interest in. You may even hesitantly admit that your kin are the sorts that relish in the news someone they dislike caught the pox; or that global warming is really a ploy by Eskimos to flood the California coastline and create a Mecca out of the Sierra Nevada mountain range.

On the contrary, you may discover you really are genuinely like them and those weekends are the most delightful times of your life. The point here is, you'll never know until you examine that elusive question, "What's really important to *me*?" in a non-superficial way, where the operative phrase is *non-superficial*. In other words, you will need to experience a deep, meaningful, sincere, thorough, and profound self-evaluation.

Excitement comes when you can stop living your life on other people's terms. The first thing you experience is freedom. Not the freedom to buy or achieve something, but the freedom to *be* something—yourself. Being free instantly creates choices that never existed before. It creates the unthinkable. Like giving up your high-powered, instant communication, six-figure job to be a schoolteacher. Or simply dropping out for a while and doing nothing except *being*. The latter implies, of course, that someone else provides food, shelter, and clothing if you haven't stored provisions away for such an idiotic, but lovely, idea.

The question now is, how do you get into this state of consciousness and still responsibly provide for those who depend on you to kill game, bring it home, and have your woman (or your man) cook up some "fixin's" for dinner? After all, the "young'ins" are depending on you for transportation (some even expect a car of their own), designer-label clothes, a cell phone or pager, and most of all, money. They are really unimpressed these days with food, shelter and clothing. That's a no-brainer. Anybody can provide that. If you really want to impress them, you simply provide the latest communication device that instantly puts them in touch with friends, rock stars, and non-stop entertainment—with a visual monitor, of course.

The way to get into this *state of consciousness* where genuine freedom of choice is available is through introspection. By carefully examining your own thoughts and feelings you discover your very own innermost values. I purposely use the term *innermost values* to distinguish them from the superficial values many of us have unconsciously adopted from our childhood, the media, or our peers. For instance, deep introspection helped a friend of mine come to the realization that his deepest and most important values had often been overshadowed by the less important value of needing to please his father. He discovered he'd been traveling a life path contrary to what he really wanted but he didn't have that awareness until he connected with *his* innermost values. Identifying his innermost values helped him make a course correction in his life path.

Likewise, many of us are so caught up in meeting the needs of our day-to-day living we don't take time to define the very tools— our innermost values—that give our efforts meaning. A fundamental purpose of this book is to assist you in this endeavor.

Chapter 1

Lessons Learned from the Man in the Moon – The New Time Paradigm

CONGRATULATIONS! You are surviving in an era that is unlike any other in the history of the world. Technology enables us to do business in the most remote corners of the globe. With the Internet, cell phones, fax machines, pagers, and computers we have created a 365-day, 24-hour society that is intense, fast-paced, and worldwide. We all agree this is *progress*, though it has come at an enormous price. We are inundated with professional responsibilities, and the conflict between our work and our personal lives is escalating.

This new environment we've created begs us, almost demands of us, to adopt a new time paradigm, one of work and personal life integration as opposed to work and personal life separation. It sounds very simple—almost too simple. But this simple shift in awareness, this new perspective, can help you create the meaning and satisfaction you've been searching for. Let's take a moment to seriously consider the power of perspective.

My flight landed in Houston, Texas. I had gone there to conduct business and to meet up with my friend, Jim Irwin. Jim had just returned home to Houston after a business trip of his own. As one of the elite Apollo 15 astronauts, Jim conducted his business in outer space. I felt almost giddy that he had invited me to dine with him while I was in Houston.

The evening finally arrived! There I was, actually sitting across the table from "The Man on the Moon." I could ask any question I wanted about this fantastic voyage, which I did. Countless questions! Enraptured, I listened to every detail of Jim's journey. I was like a schoolboy listening to tales of adventure from my super-hero. I remember asking him, "Jim, of all the many experiences you had on this trip, what do you consider to be the single most exciting?"

He thought for a moment, and then responded, "That's a tough question." After several more moments his eyes lit up and a visible wave of enthusiasm spread across his face as he said, "I'll tell you what one of the most exciting things was. It was to be orbiting the moon and see the Earth rising! To see our magnificent planet as a small, blue–and–white marble is an experience I will never forget."

Then he said something I will never forget. "If you want to get life's problems and challenges in their proper perspective you should try it. Orbit the moon and watch the Earth rise. Something about the experience shrinks all of your problems down to size."

Jim left his earthly boundaries and gained a fresh outlook. He returned from his journey altered and energized with a new outlook on what his time on "Spaceship Earth" could be. He was motivated to spend the remainder of his life in service to others.

This was a lesson of immeasurable worth for me. I now call it the *principle of perspective*. Sometimes we are so close to situations, conditions, and life routines we fail to perceive or appreciate their infinite possibilities. A new perspective helps us discover our options.

Perspective is how we see things. A paradigm is a patterned way of thinking and seeing things or, a habitual perspective. When Jim Irwin saw our planet from a fresh perspective he was transformed. Our Earth appeared so small to him, he could reach out and cover it with his thumbnail. This compelling moment, among other experiences, moved him to face the big question, "What's really important?" In the process of discovering his answer, he was changed. His previous patterned way of thinking and seeing things, his old paradigm, was gone forever. From his space voyage forward he was committed to serving others. The point here is, your *perspective* can change in an instant by your own realization of what's truly important to you!

In his book, *To Rule the Night*, Jim says, "I came back from the Apollo 15 flight to find it had changed my life. Before, I was a nuts-and-bolts type, a technician, one who was too busy with details to be really concerned over the needs and feelings of other men and women on earth. Now I have a new perception and a new appreciation for this spaceship we call earth. It has been a real spiritual awakening. I think I am a person who loves all men, and God has given me a strong desire and compulsion to share my life with them."

Wouldn't it be great if we could all travel in space and return with a fresh perspective, a new paradigm of our very own—complete with a deeper appreciation for our planet and the people we share it with? Well, thanks to the Russian space program you can! For a mere $20 million dollars you too can travel to space! What a great opportunity!

But if you are like me and you have other plans for your spare change, there is still a way to awaken to the truth about who you are, what you want, and how to get it even in our expanding chaotic environment. Keep reading!

The Basic Building Blocks of Our Life Experience

Life is made up of events and activities. An event is anything that happens. Anything! Events can have the magnitude of a major catastrophe such as a world war or they can be as simple as a mosquito landing on your arm. Some events happen *independently* of us and some events happen *to* us.

An activity is a special kind of event. An activity is an event that is driven through the expenditure of our physical, mental, and emotional energy. Many events occur independently of us while an *activity* is executed *by* us. An activity is something *we* do. Even sleeping is an activity.

> *Many events occur independently of us while an activity is executed by us. An activity is something we do.*

From the day we draw our first breath of life until the moment we die, we are executing activities on a nonstop basis. Let's take a closer look at the truth about activities. Some are:

- Physical
- Mental
- Subliminal
- Long in duration
- Short in duration

Some of long duration can have little consequence. Sometimes, those of short duration can have long lasting consequences.

Activities are never neutral. They enhance or detract from our lives by changing the quality for better or worse. The following statements illustrate this point:

- Concentration of power permits us to fully experience an activity.
- Those activities that align with our innermost values give us a sense of satisfaction greater than those that don't.
- Activities creatively arranged in a sequence can culminate in the achievement of a desired goal.
- Negative activities repeated over and over again can erode our well-being.
- Positive activities repeated over and over again can make us stronger and improve our well-being.
- Activities repeated over and over again become habits—habits can be our greatest servants or our worst task-masters.
- When we choose to execute certain activities, we simultaneously exclude others—it's about choice.
- Some activities can be frightening.

As long as we are alive, we are doing activities. To become more efficient and effective at executing these non-stop activities, many of us have tried to learn time-management skills. In some ways the phrase *time management* is misleading because most individuals are under the subtle, but very real, misconception that managing time means managing the clock. The truth is, we cannot manage the clock. It will continue to tick off the hours and the minutes no matter how hard we try to speed it up or slow it down.

What we can do is take responsibility for managing our most important activities. This approach is more in line with Albert Einstein's definition of time, which is: "Time is the occurrence of events one after another." So then, managing time is really about managing, even orchestrating, the occurrence of activities in our lives.

There is absolutely no question that managing activities is harder to do than ever before. There are two reasons for this. First, how we *measure* events and activities has *not* changed. We still measure or track them according to *clock* time, which is constant, moving progressively from the past through the present into the future. Second, how we *experience* events and activities *has* changed. Now, more than ever before, significant events occur with more frequency. With machine gun–like intensity they are more intrusive, simultaneous, spontaneous, global, urgent, and unexpected. Priorities shift and change throughout the day, conflicting with one another, creating personal and workplace turbulence.

Today, more events happen and more activities are available for our choosing. That's the problem! It isn't that we have *fewer* minutes in the day. Our predicament is that we have *more* activities to handle.

> *Today more events happen and more activities are available for our choosing. That's the problem! It isn't that we have fewer minutes in the day. Our predicament is that we have more activities to handle.*

In short, we are expected to:

Increase performance…
> while managing *more* activities…
> in *shorter* periods of time…
> in the midst of *uncertainty*…
> with *fewer* resources…
> as we strive to *continuously* learn…
while *balancing* work and personal life.

Most people are having a great deal of difficulty coping with the dilemma of *"time compression."* The challenges are unprecedented. Like the manager I know who went on vacation for three weeks and when she came back she had 2600 e-mail messages.

As the time between cause and effect gets shorter, and the number of events with which we deal increases, it impacts everything we do. The pressures are enormous and continue to build. Some days are so intense they seem completely unmanageable. One executive who manages one hundred employees said to me, "I was so overwhelmed yesterday, I went home, sat in a chair, and cried."

For many people, the natural response to these new challenges is working faster and faster and longer and longer. If people who are doing this had speedometers like automobiles, we would see many are pushing the human machine to the red line. They are operating dangerously near burnout or even breakdown! People in this state use cliché statements such as "I'm drowning," "I have too much on my plate," "I have too many balls in the air," "I'm working my fingers to the bone," "I've bitten off more than I can chew," and "I don't have a life." When we operate in this state, stress goes up and the quality of life goes down.

So here we are, caught in the crossfire of technology, speed, transformational change, uncertainty, and the expectation to do more with less. How does one deal with too many activities, fewer resources, life balance, and still meet the expectations of higher performance on the job?

For decades, time and life management experts have been recommending we attack the problem by dividing our "self" into the various roles we perform and then scheduling our days accordingly. For example, I am a husband, father, grandfather, son, brother, uncle, business owner, speaker, mentor, author, citizen, neighbor, etc. WHEW! I feel exhausted! I feel fragmented when I consider all those different divisions of myself and that's not even a complete list.

This approach works for some but most of us are frustrated and overwhelmed, even paralyzed by what it means to think in terms of "me, the marketing VP," and "me, the soccer mom," and "me, the caregiver daughter," and "me, the good neighbor," and "me, the voter," and on and on and on.

Remember the old saying, "Divide and Conquer"? The concept is that you can conquer or overcome the smaller, individual, divided pieces. And it works! Now take a minute to really think that through. By dividing yourself into all the different roles you perform, who did you just set up to be conquered and overcome? The hazard of fragmenting yourself in this way is chaos and ultimately the feeling of utter failure.

In the new time paradigm, it is critical you approach life as one complete "you"—an integrated, whole individual pouring your heart and energy into your various activities. The concept of *divide and conquer* is still valid in the new paradigm but we use it on our activities not on ourselves. It makes no sense to fragment and thereby dilute the only energy source we have available to accomplish those activities.

When we divide and conquer our *activities* there are only four fundamental groups: self activities, family activities, work activities and service activities. These groups form the basis of our very existence. Each of us is an entity (self) with a family (whether we know them or not) who must have means with which to subsist (whether we work for it or let society provide it) and we affect everyone around us (whether we contribute positively or hermit ourselves away in a hole). Our life, from birth to death, is made by the conscious or unconscious integration of these four areas.

Clearly, managing our lives in the midst of chaos requires new levels of self-management skills. We must become better *choosers*, better *arrangers*, better *doers*, better *changers*, and better *concentrators*. We must also become more *intuitive* and *versatile*. In short, we need to become empowered self-managers.

Yes, it was easier to balance work and personal life in the sixties, the seventies, and even the eighties. We drew an imaginary line between the two and that was that. We left work and went home to the family. Sometimes, but rarely, we would take work home. There was not a multiplicity of electronic devices to facilitate work worries after hours. If somebody did work all the time, it was his or her personality not the environment that was driving it. In those times, only some medical doctors were on call 24 hours per day.

Now, nearly everyone is involved in an integrated work-life 24-hour day. In this global 365-day, 24-hour society, pretending the line between work and personal life still exists is to be out of touch with reality.

So here we are! The new paradigm is simply this: We live in an era of work-life integration, as opposed to work-life separation. By accepting it and understanding it, you can now begin creating that heretofore elusive *work-life quality and balance* you've only had the courage to wish for.

> *The new paradigm is simply this: We live in an era of work-life integration as opposed to work-life separation.*

There are thousands of recipes for success that consist of complicated habits and rules and policies and laws. In the new time paradigm there is only one rule: "See yourself as yourself, one complete whole individual, and live life with all your heart!"

> **In the new time paradigm there is only one rule:**
> **See yourself as yourself, one complete whole**
> **individual, and live life with all your heart!**

But what is the *work-life quality and balance* people are talking about that so few seem to achieve?

Life Quality is the *sense of satisfaction* we experience when our activities are congruent with our innermost values. These values characterize life activities involving *self, family, work,* and *service*. When we live congruent with our innermost values, our life has purpose, meaning, enjoyment, aliveness, joy, satisfaction, and contribution to others. We experience very little, or no overwhelm and burnout when we are congruent within ourselves.

Life Balance is achieved by appropriately allocating time and energy to the activities in each of the four main categories I mentioned earlier:

- **Self**: managing our physical, mental, and spiritual well-being
- **Family**: managing the mutual needs and desires of those we care for
- **Work**: managing the professional responsibilities that provide income
- **Service**: managing our personal contributions to others

Life Management is the process of consciously living the activities that are congruent with your innermost values.

Innermost Values are the core beliefs that define who you are when you are being honest within yourself and authentic in your relationships with others. Innermost values include the following criteria. They:

- Benefit self and others
- Are a reflection of who we are
- Create alignment of purpose/people
- Come with surety (validated by the heart)
- Respect and value individual and group dignity

- Create inner meaning and motivation about work
- Involve empathy, compassion, humility, and love
- Create physical, mental, and spiritual well-being
- Create inner peace in one's self (stability and centeredness)
- Are right brain sourced, such as nudges, intuition, and insights
- Are a natural desire to help others grow, learn, and succeed

Notice I am offering only criteria for innermost values. It is left up to you to determine if they are appropriate for you. Keep in mind that you can learn values from outside sources as well. These however, become yours only when you internalize and naturally live them.

One way to begin the discovery of our authentic selves is through a personal inventory. I was a retailer for many years. Once a year we took a complete physical inventory. Every year, without exception, some of our inventory was missing. A personal inventory will help you clarify what's missing in your life from a quality perspective. Then, with more clarity you can begin to fill in the gaps.

Chapter 2

Coffee, Tea, or the Sea? – Taking a Personal Inventory

It was a gray overcast morning at the Seattle/Tacoma Airport. I had reservations for a flight to Anchorage, Alaska. For some reason I felt a little uneasy about the trip. Nevertheless, I buckled into my seat and tried to relax. We were flying on a propeller airplane so when we reached the beginning of the runway the pilot carefully revved up each engine, one at a time, just to be sure everything was working.

Take–off time! The engines roared with full power and we lifted off. We were only a few hundred feet off the ground when we suddenly lost power. The airplane seemed to be just gliding along with barely enough airspeed to keep us flying. It was too late to abort so the pilot carefully banked the airplane and headed toward the water of the Puget Sound. White knuckles popped up on the backs of my hands. We were slowly sinking toward the sea.

A flight attendant came rushing down the aisle to where I was seated. I looked up into his face for some sort of reassurance. His face was flushed and nervous. He looked at me and shook his head. Reaching up he pulled a handle and a life raft dropped at my feet. We were going to hit the water.

I quickly did an analysis of the odds for my survival. They weren't very good. We were about to experience what the airlines refer to in pre-take-off instructions as "a water landing." By interpretation that means a crash. Friends who had faced life-threatening experiences told me your life flashes in front of you. They were right! It was happening to me. There were no thoughts about material things—only relationships. What's really important loomed up in my mind. What have I accomplished up to this point?

What am I remorseful about? If I survive, what would I like to do with my life?

Moments later the first officer and the flight attendant were attempting to open the aircraft door. I became increasingly nervous. My nose was pressed against the window. I noticed oil slick on the water, then luggage, then people in the water. Our crew was attempting to drop life rafts to the survivors of the flight that had taken off just ahead of us. It had ditched into the Puget Sound. I'm not exactly sure when I realized that our plane was fine, but I feel certain many of the people on that other flight had feelings similar to my own.

Experiences such as these tend to create a state of personal inventory taking. They give us a sense of clarity. They give us the resolve to do a better job managing our lives. They help us to fast focus on the big picture. We often have the realization that as long as we have the gift of life, every minute is a new beginning.

> *We often have the realization that as long as we have the gift of life, every minute is a new beginning.*

The truth is, we needn't wait for a crisis to take an inventory. If we are hungering for a better quality of life and a new beginning, taking a personal inventory is a good place to start. A personal inventory, honestly taken, is a reality check. It is the first step toward a more fulfilling life. The realizations gained from an inventory can become a solid foundation for decision-making.

The Big Picture

Clearly, one way to take an inventory is through a life threatening experience. It is certainly poignant but not altogether necessary. You can focus on the big picture of your own life without a harrowing life-threatening experience and you can do it without going to the moon. Sidney B. Simon, Ed.D. outlines the approach in his book *Meeting Yourself Halfway*, 1974.

Instructions: Along the line below from your Birth to your predicted Death locate where you are now (the present place) and place a dot. If you are an optimist, you might assume you'll live to be at least 100 years old. Now write an age number over this dot. (Keep it private, if appropriate!) This line is your Lifeline.

Birth_____**Death**

To the left of your "present dot," write a few simple words that represent what you believe you have accomplished thus far in your life. To the right of your "present dot," write two or three significant things you believe you would like to personally accomplish before you die. For example, one of the activities I want to accomplish before I die is to write an essay for and about each of our children. The intent of the essay is to let them know how deeply I love them. The essays will express what I admire about their character and talents and why they have meant so much in my life. I am currently working on those essays. I've found it to be a very fulfilling life-quality experience. I feel a sense of urgency to compile the work. In some cases, your words or phrases might be personal growth, scientific exploration, or service to others.

The words of your lifeline also reveal a pattern of purpose and meaning in the overall theme of your life. This theme provides a guideline to determine whether or not your activities are congruent with your theme. See if you can decipher the "theme of your life" from the words you have written along your lifeline.

A Personal Inventory

Let's go further with your personal inventory. The previous exercise gives you the big picture of your life from 40,000 feet. An additional inventory method is through an personal assessment. The following exercise is designed to assess the *state of your life* at this time. Evaluate the extent to which each of the qualities below exists in your life. Use a scale of 0 (lowest) to 10 (highest) to evaluate yourself. Then total each column.

Work-Life Quality – A Personal Assessment

Enthusiasm	_____	Sadness	_____
Satisfaction	_____	Pain	_____
Peace	_____	Boredom	_____
Wellness	_____	Fear	_____
Security	_____	Overwhelm	_____
Happiness	_____	Depression	_____
Love	_____	Anger	_____
Meaning	_____	Anxiety	_____
Wisdom	_____	Stress	_____
Total	_____	Total	_____

As you review the results of this personal inventory, please do not view the left-hand column as positive and the right-hand column as negative. If you are experiencing emotions from the right hand column it doesn't necessarily mean your life does not have quality and balance.

Remember, I defined life quality as the sense of satisfaction you experience when your activities are congruent with your innermost values. For example, if you are currently a caregiver for an elderly parent, you may be experiencing sadness, pain, anxiety, and stress. These emotions are probably appropriate for such a situation. At the same time, the activity of caring for a loved one is congruent with your innermost values. Life quality does not mean we are happy every minute of the day. Life involves a variety of feelings and emotions, appropriate to the situation we may be experiencing. Also, we've asked you to use a scale of 0-10 to assess the extent to which each of the qualities exists in your life.

The numbers are only intended as a guide for helping you assess the state of your life so don't take them too literally.

Based on your results (the totals in each column) and keeping foremost in your mind that life quality is determined by how congruent your actions are with your innermost values, select a category below that best fits your overall work-life quality. The quality of your life is determined by you. Whatever you choose is what's important to you!

1. _____ FANTASTIC! It can't get much better, incredible maybe. YAHOO!
2. _____ GREAT! There are some changes I need to make to have it be fantastic.
3. _____ GOOD! There is reason for concern regarding a significant issue I am unwilling to confront.
4. _____ HOLDING ON! I feel I am moving, but in the wrong (or right) direction.
5. _____ MISERABLE! I feel stuck, victimized, and not in control of my life. Life sucks!

No matter how you evaluated yourself, there is something cathartic and freeing about telling the truth. It creates the space for change to occur where desired and appropriate. When such is the case, it usually begins with the introspective process of looking inside of yourself.

A Transformational Experience

Perhaps the best route to our inner selves is to face a major life crisis. Most of us will be *blessed* with one or more during our lifetime, whether we choose to or not. It took a challenging experience in my own life to deepen my appreciation of what is really important to me. It was years after I had learned the *principle of perspective* from Jim Irwin, the Apollo 15 Astronaut, that I fully experienced its impact on my own transformational experience. I learned that problems and challenges help us gain that perspective.

In 1986 my family and I went through an unimaginable and stressful change in our lives. We had enjoyed a successful family business for 25 years. For 15 of those years I was president. Confident in our prosperity, we gambled on some big risks. Those risks proved to be a disaster and after three very difficult years, the bank justifiably called our loan due. We lost all of our financial resources. I will never forget the day we sold our last asset—our home—and gave the money to the bank. It was a very emotional time. I felt like a loser! I felt guilty, thinking how I had disappointed our employees, our vendors, and my family. We had no assets to show for our 25 years of hard, dedicated work.

I was 51 years old—not the best time in life to be broke! I looked around, and began to notice time-related things I had never noticed before. Some little lines and some not–so–little lines appeared in my skin. I became aware that the majority of company presidents were 10 to 15 years younger than I was. I envied many of my friends who had retired. They had made it. I was starting over.

I recognized that starting over financially I would be competing in the workplace with bright, energetic, much-younger people—entrepreneurs who were the ages of my children. I felt a huge incongruity between my condition in life and the time in which I was living. I was a time traveler on Spaceship Earth who was out of sync with my time. I was displaced. My life was out of balance. It was at this point that my appreciation deepened for what's really important. I began to plan all of my activities carefully. I also became grateful for the challenges we faced because through them our entire family was transformed. Relationships deepened. I now relish each day with its unlimited possibilities for quality of life.

A life crisis has the potential to tear an individual or a family apart. It also has the potential to help us grow and bring the family together. It all depends on the attitudes of the people involved. In our case, the entire family increased in wisdom and was drawn closer together. In fact, our financial challenge generated one of the highest points in my entire life.

Having lost all of our financial resources I had accepted a job with another company. This was a major change for me. I had always been in business for myself. I could have stayed and retired with the company, but I was unhappy working for a major corporation. My job also kept me on the east coast and my family was all out west. With the support of my wife, I decided to quit my job and go back into business for myself. I was in my mid-fifties and had no capital. We gave the company two weeks notice and headed west.

Shortly after our arrival, our four children invited us to a family dinner at our daughter's home. After dinner they handed me a gift to unwrap. It was a handsome briefcase. "Open it up," they said. I did. It was filled with one thousand dollars in crisp, brand new, one-dollar bills. It was only one thousand dollars in cash, but to me it was worth millions in emotional capital. It was difficult for them to come up with that much money at this time in their lives and I knew it. To this day I'm still energized by their expression of love and confidence in our new beginning. It was, and still is, one of the highest moments of my life.

Since that time, I've discovered that some of the most successful people I know have been challenged. They have been *highly* challenged! Sometimes it was financial, sometimes it was physical, sometimes it was emotional, and often it was a combination of all three. Those individuals are successful because they did not let their challenges defeat them. Instead they used their hardships as a springboard for new directions in life.

If you are currently undergoing a crisis of your own, you can resolve to learn from it. Your situation can be a catalyst for going deeper inside yourself, where you've never gone before, to look for meaning and a new perspective. Finding your own perspective of what's really important to you will give direction and motivation to begin managing your life in a way that is full and rewarding, even exhilarating.

And if you don't have a challenging lesson looming in your life at the moment, here is one more tool that will help you uncover what is truly important to you.

An Intellectual Inventory (long survey)

This survey is designed for you to evaluate the quality of your life in four major areas:

1. **Self**: Those activities involving your personal well-being; the balanced integration of body, mind, and spirit.
2. **Family**: Those activities involving significant family relationships; extended and otherwise.
3. **Work**: Those activities primarily related to work life or earning a living.
4. **Service**: Those activities involving contribution to others outside of work and family

Each of the four categories in this inventory consists of five statements. The instructions below pertain to the entire survey.

First, consider each statement in a category and **focus on the bolded words**. Determine the **importance** of the bolded phrase to your life quality and circle the number on the scale (from 1 to 4) to indicate your answer; (1), not important and (4), extremely important.

Second, read the complete statements in each category and determine your level of agreement or your level of commitment as it applies to that particular statement. Circle the appropriate number on the scale (from 1 to 5) to indicate your choice.

Third, multiply your *importance* number times your *agreement* number and record your total. Add your scores in each category to obtain the subtotal of that category.

Respond to the following statements based on your experience and/or behavior in your personal and professional life.

A Personal Work-Life Survey – SELF

Scale of Importance: 1–Not Important 2–Slightly Important 3–Quite Important 4–Extremely Important

Scale of Agreement: 1–Strongly Disagree 2–Disagree 3–Neutral 4–Agree 5–Strongly Agree

1. I devote sufficient effort to my **physical well-being**.
   Importance: 1   2   3   4
   Agreement: 1   2   3   4   5
   Total: _____

2. I have a **personal hobby that provides me with adequate relaxation**.
   Importance: 1   2   3   4
   Agreement: 1   2   3   4   5
   Total: _____

3. I actively embrace **personal growth** opportunities.
   Importance: 1   2   3   4
   Agreement: 1   2   3   4   5
   Total: _____

4. I actively practice a **religious and/or spiritual discipline**.
   Importance: 1   2   3   4
   Agreement: 1   2   3   4   5
   Total: _____

5. Overall, I feel **integrated and balanced in terms of body, mind, and spirit**.
   Importance: 1   2   3   4
   Agreement: 1   2   3   4   5
   Total: _____

SELF SUBTOTAL _____   **INTERPRETATION** _____
(Shown on pages 32-35)

A Personal Work-Life Survey – FAMILY

Scale of Importance: 1–Not Important 2–Slightly Important 3–Quite Important 4–Extremely Important

Scale of Agreement: 1–Strongly Disagree 2–Disagree 3–Neutral 4–Agree 5–Strongly Agree

1. I experience **quality relationship and communication with my spouse, partner, or significant other**.
   Importance: 1   2   3   4
   Agreement: 1   2   3   4   5
   Total: _____

2. I experience **quality relationship and communication with other significant family members, (children, parents, in-laws, cousins, etc.)**.
   Importance: 1   2   3   4
   Agreement: 1   2   3   4   5
   Total: _____

3. I devote **sufficient quality time with my family** to achieve balance with my work responsibilities.
   Importance: 1   2   3   4
   Agreement: 1   2   3   4   5
   Total: _____

4. I **proactively resolve family conflicts, problems, or crises as they occur**.
   Importance: 1   2   3   4
   Agreement: 1   2   3   4   5
   Total: _____

5. Overall, I am **satisfied with both the time devoted to and the quality of my family (or interpersonal) relationships**.
   Importance: 1   2   3   4
   Agreement: 1   2   3   4   5
   Total: _____

FAMILY SUBTOTAL _____   **INTERPRETATION** _____
(Shown on pages 32-35)

A Personal Work-Life Survey – WORK

Scale of Importance: 1–Not Important 2–Slightly Important 3–Quite Important 4–Extremely Important

Scale of Agreement: 1–Strongly Disagree 2–Disagree 3–Neutral 4–Agree 5–Strongly Agree

1. My **work is personally meaningful** to me.
    Importance: 1   2   3   4
    Agreement: 1   2   3   4   5
    Total: _____

2. I **exercise maximum self-management in the performance of my job**.
    Importance: 1   2   3   4
    Agreement: 1   2   3   4   5
    Total: _____

3. I am **very competent for the work that I do**.
    Importance: 1   2   3   4
    Agreement: 1   2   3   4   5
    Total: _____

4. I am **creative and innovative as required by my work** situations.
    Importance: 1   2   3   4
    Agreement: 1   2   3   4   5
    Total: _____

5. Overall, I am **clear about my short and long term career goals and my plan to achieve them**.
    Importance: 1   2   3   4
    Agreement: 1   2   3   4   5
    Total: _____

WORK SUBTOTAL _____   **INTERPRETATION** _____
(Shown on pages 32-35)

A Personal Work-Life Survey – SERVICE

Scale of Importance: 1–Not Important 2–Slightly Important 3–Quite Important 4–Extremely Important

Scale of Agreement: 1–Strongly Disagree 2–Disagree 3–Neutral 4–Agree 5–Strongly Agree

1. I am aware of how I would like most to **contribute to society or others,** i.e., money, time, support, etc.
   Importance: 1   2   3   4
   Agreement: 1   2   3   4   5
   Total: _____

2. I devote **sufficient time in service to others,** i.e., community, religious, recreational, support, etc.
   Importance: 1   2   3   4
   Agreement: 1   2   3   4   5
   Total: _____

3. I feel I **make a difference in the lives of others**.
   Importance: 1   2   3   4
   Agreement: 1   2   3   4   5
   Total: _____

4. I **contribute to societal organizations in proportion to my own monetary resources,** i.e., tithing, contributions, etc.
   Importance: 1   2   3   4
   Agreement: 1   2   3   4   5
   Total: _____

5. I feel a **natural desire to contribute to the welfare and well-being of others**.
   Importance: 1   2   3   4
   Agreement: 1   2   3   4   5
   Total: _____

SERVICE SUBTOTAL _____   **INTERPRETATION** _____
(Shown on pages 32-35)

Finally, add the subtotals for each category on the previous pages to obtain a total score.

Subtotals

Self   _____
Family   _____
Work   _____
Service   _____

Total   _____

The highest possible score in each category is 100. At a glance, you can quickly evaluate the quality and level of activity you experience in each category. Look more closely at each category. Be sure to notice what is working for you. Also, begin to notice any gaps between how your life is at present and how you would like it to be. Read through the following descriptions and select one that best fits your overall personal evaluation for each of the four areas of your life. Only *you* can determine exactly what your number totals mean.

Category Description One

Fantastic! Incredible even! You feel it couldn't be better!

Category Description Two

Things are great and you know with a little work the quality could get better.

Category Description Three

Things are okay but there is reason for concern. Your life is always changing and the quality of life goes up and down.

Category Description Four

Life is a struggle the majority of the time. You are either on your way up or on your way down. You're just never sure which way you are moving.

Category Description Five

Life is a constant battle and you feel like you're always losing.

If descriptions four or five best characterize your situation in one or more categories, you might want to decide whether significant change is appropriate in your life at this time. If change is important, you will need to make a dedicated effort in both prioritization and commitment to the types of activities you are presently doing. It will also probably involve dealing with a situation in your life that will require a significant personal change. If change is not important or vital at this point in your life, then be willing to accept the consequences of the quality you experience without feeling victimized.

Closing the Gaps or Interpreting Your Scores

You just chose a category description based on the analysis you made of each. But the real answers for improving your life quality lie in the results of each individual statement. Go back again and pay particular attention to the statements where your results reveal a significant gap between the importance of a particular value to you and the amount of effort you put into actualizing that value. For instance, the first evaluation statement was:

*I devote sufficient effort to my **physical well-being**.*

Most of us would probably rank physical well-being as *extremely important.* After all, if we don't feel healthy how can we accomplish or enjoy anything else? *Extremely important* is evaluated as a numerical score of 4.

For the sake of our example, let's say I really don't give sufficient effort to my physical well-being because whenever the urge to exercise comes along I find some excuse. In addition, I eat on the go and I don't get nearly enough sleep. Looking at my life I determine that I give very little effort to my physical well-being so I must disagree or strongly disagree with the above evaluation statement. *Strongly disagree* has a numerical score of 1 or a total score of 4 x 1 = 4.

The highest possible rating on any statement is 20 (4 Extremely Important x 5 Strongly Agree). In this example my score is 4 out of 20. That score tells me that my actions are not congruent with what I believe to be important. In fact, it is a huge difference between the two!

Several years ago, I came to the conclusion that sufficient exercise was not integrated into my life. If I didn't do something about it, I was headed for some form of breakdown, given the pace I keep. So, I enrolled in a health club with my wife. I use her often to keep me going to the club when I don't feel motivated and vice versa. I had no idea how much physical exercise relaxes all the tension I experience during a busy, stressful workday. I even take my exercise clothing and shoes on my regular business trips. The key for me—make up your mind and "Just Do It!"

On the other hand, there may be a statement in the survey that expresses a value that really isn't very important to you so the possible high score of 20 doesn't tell the *whole* story. We'll do one more example so you understand how to interpret your scores. Let's say my innermost value concerning service is that service is more than just donating money. We'll use the statement:

"I contribute to societal organizations in proportion to my own monetary resources, i.e., tithing, contributions, etc."

Because I believe that service is important and that it can be given in a lot of different ways, not just money, I rate *contribute to societal organizations in proportion to my own monetary resources* as slightly important. *Slightly important* has a numerical score of 2. Because I contribute my service in the form of personal time, I strongly disagree with the statement. *Strongly disagree* has a numerical score of 1 or 2 x 1 = 2. In this example, my score of 2 is exactly the same as the importance I place on that action. No gap. This indicates that the importance of this action to me, and the amount of effort I give it, is congruent.

Now that you've gone back over each statement in the long survey to assess specific areas of your life, step back and take a look at the *big picture* of your life. Consider also the results of your Personal Survey and the things you may be learning from any challenges you have experienced or may be experiencing now. What are they trying to tell you about yourself? Now, read through the following descriptions and choose the one that best describes your overall life quality and consider the suggestions for maintaining or achieving the quality you desire.

Overall Life Quality Description One

Life is great! You take responsibility for creating the priorities of the activities in your life. As a result, you understand what is important to you and your family, and you align family, work, and service according to these values. As long as you openly embrace personal transformation as a requirement for adapting to a rapidly changing world, you will be consistently in this category.

Overall Life Quality Description Two

Life is very good, although there may be some imbalance or even priorities that are on hold at the present time. In order to keep things at least at this level, continue to learn and grow from your life experiences since the other three categories may *force* adaptation and adjustment. If you don't continually experience personal growth, you will slip to a lower description.

Overall Life Quality Description Three

Life is okay. If you truly desire an expanded quality of life you will have to take decisive steps in personal transformation. You will have to confront an issue of major proportion that will have consequences you cannot control. It is the barrier to an expanded quality of life. If you don't choose to resolve it, your life circumstances will force resolution sooner or later. You may or may not like the outcome.

Overall Life Quality Description Four

Life is a challenge. There are high points, particularly with people and activities that are supportive and of value to you. However, you will have to look deep inside yourself to discover what you truly value, beyond the expectations of society or even your family. It is only from this inner perspective that you can begin to reconstruct your life to the expanded quality you may desire. Remember, it is easy to slip into the description below, if you simply maintain the status quo!

Overall Life Quality Description Five

Life is a constant series of crises, some major and some minor. Most likely your physical health and overall well-being is affected in some significant way. The only way to initiate change is through in-depth personal and probably spiritual transformation. These will either be brought about by your own proactive effort or by one of the constant crises you regularly experience. It may also be initiated by illness, an accident, loss of employment, a family crisis, or an interpersonal crisis. If you consider your present life circumstances to be undesirable, as a statement of reflection, consider this: *You create your own reality right down to the detailed circumstances of everything you experience.*

Summary

Now that you've finished the evaluations in this section, what have you discovered about yourself? Have you had any of those "A-HA" moments?

Perhaps you learned that you are satisfied because your life is brimming with quality. You realize there isn't a lot you want to change. Perhaps you are feeling a little disappointed but still hopefully determined. In being honest with yourself, you sometimes discover bigger gaps than you expect to find. You know with a few adjustments, more contentment and meaning are just around the corner if you are willing to roll up your sleeves and get to work. Perhaps you feel utterly disappointed and completely overwhelmed with the amount of work needed to bring your life in line with your ideals. And, just maybe, you relate to all of the statements above. You feel great about some parts of your life, determined to work on other parts, and scared to death to even admit to some of it.

Wherever you are, don't stop now! You've completed the hardest part. Everything gets better from here on out. And it all begins with the principles you'll learn in the next chapter!

Chapter 3

It's Your Life! –
Taking Responsibility for Your Life

"Our true home, our rightful sense of belonging and security, is found not in the outer world but within ourselves."

James Ballard

Before taking action to address any gaps you may have discovered, you first have to take responsibility for your present circumstances and conditions. In a phrase, you must first take responsibility for your life.

Taking responsibility for your life is such a simple phrase. But what does it really mean? It means claiming ownership for literally everything that has happened to you to the present moment. For example, I proudly take ownership for earning a Ph.D. and creating a successful scientific career with international recognition. However, I'm not so proud to own the events leading to my divorce several years ago. In fact, I sometimes find myself attempting to divert conversations to something more favorable about me. I recently got a telephone call from a friend that I had not seen in nine years. He wanted to reconnect and have lunch. During the course of our conversation, he asked, "How's your wife and kid?" Red flag! So, two sentences later I said, "I'm divorced, remarried, and have *two* daughters now; both girls with my former wife." There, I got it all out, in one sentence. What's his opinion of me now? Does he still want to have lunch? Is he still interested in how it all happened and who's fault it was? However, once I exposed everything, I felt a tremendous sense of relief.

To claim ownership, I must acknowledge both the favorable and unfavorable aspects of my life and use both as learning experiences. Let's take that one step further. Claiming ownership *in the most constructive way* means to readily acknowledge both aspects *without self-judgment or evaluation.* Constructive ownership without blame, fault, or guilt provides the basis for constructive change and new learning.

> **Constructive ownership, without judgment, evaluation, or guilt provides the basis for constructive change and new learning.**

Constructive change, or setting a new direction to improve your life quality, will probably require you to define and confront an issue or situation you have been avoiding. It is likely that it will also require a transformational experience, with respect to that issue or situation in order to have your redesigned plan be effective.

For example, taking time for *deep introspection* with respect to one's own role in a divorce provides the learning necessary for not repeating the same behavior. Deep introspection allows understanding to occur at a visceral level and it often redefines our perspective about life. If we simply persist in seeing the other person as the sole problem in such situations then we righteously view ourselves as a martyr or victim. This position is the essence of denying responsibility for one's life. Unfortunately, there are too many people who support us in this state of victimization instead of helping us take responsibility for our part in the sequence of events that led to situations we are not proud of, namely a separation or a divorce.

Am I Responsible for My Present Situation?

In the previous chapter, you had the opportunity, using several tools, to evaluate the overall state of your life. In one survey you were asked to determine your personal state of being on a scale ranging from FANTASTIC to MISERABLE. That evaluation was not intended to be judgmental. That is, it is not necessarily good to be fantastic or bad if you are miserable, unless you judge it to be so. Not judging how your life is, allows you to clearly *see* and *own* the way it is. It provides a basis for comparing it with how you'd like it to be.

The interpretations you made as a result of the evaluations probably created a gap between how your life is now and some desired state you'd like in the future. This is called a "gap analysis." Let me demonstrate what I mean.

Spending quality time with my two daughters from my previous marriage is important to me. To do so meant I would have to make a crucial decision with respect to my business travel. More precisely, I would have to travel less on weekends throughout the year. Here's the dilemma. Conferences and speaking engagements are commonly held on weekends and they are the most vital marketing and income producing opportunities for my business. This is what I meant earlier when I stated that creating the quality and balance you desire will require you to define and confront a situation you may have been avoiding. So where do I start reconciling what appears to be a dilemma?

I began by identifying my innermost values; those that define who I am when I am honest within myself and authentic in my relationship to others; those that endure over time and go beyond short-term recognition, advancement, and reward. In this situation, the value for me is the extreme importance I place on *family*. That meant that all my professional activities would have to be rearranged around quality time with my daughters. The arrangement or promise I made with myself and with them is that I would not be away from them more than four weekends a year. This is what I meant earlier (page 32), when I indicated that an enhanced quality of life will require a significant personal change.

> *Innermost values define who you are when you are honest within yourself and authentic in your relationship to others. They are enduring over time, and transcend recognition, advancement, or reward.*

I made that promise several years ago and have accomplished it ever since. In fact, I've even added to that promise by having them with me during extended holiday periods and three weeks during the summer. My intent is to continually find *more* creative ways of spending time with them, e.g., accompanying me on selected business trips on weekends.

Lessons Learned from Taking Responsibility

We learn our greatest lessons when we take responsibility for unfavorable events in our lives. As long as I persisted in believing that my work required extensive weekend travel I also viewed myself as being victimized by it. When I decided that I create my own reality, then change instantly began to occur and I felt empowered to do just that.

An important lesson I learned by keeping my promise to my daughters is that I am not indispensable at work. There are others in my organization just as skillful at speaking and facilitating as I am. I did not need to lose business if I had the humility to coach and promote them as well as myself. The two are mutually compatible and more successful in the long run.

An even deeper lesson I came to understand is that my dilemma over wanting to spend more time with my daughters and not wanting to lose business was all based on my ego. My ego-need to be the star was based upon my belief of being indispensable and the *only* one who could best deliver the message. Certainly others around me couldn't possibly be as good as I. Remember, I also said earlier (page 34) that expanded quality would require confronting a personal issue of major proportion.

Well, this is it for me. As of this writing, I still don't have it quite mastered, but I am significantly more humble than I used to be.

As I learned to deal with my ego, I could see that not only are others as good as I am, with certain types of audiences, they are better! At first this realization felt like a threat. Then, I felt relief for my own physical, mental, and spiritual well-being. And my daughters had their dad.

I am now patterning my speaking and conference engagements the way Tiger Woods appears to schedule his tournaments. Instead of appearing in every event on the Professional Golfer's Association (PGA) Tour, he selectively picks the *majors* and other significant events that align with his goals. Isn't it interesting that he has been the number one golfer in the world and earned the most money over the last four consecutive years through 2002!

Permanent Change Begins with Taking Responsibility

The crucial message of this chapter is that permanent change begins with taking 100 percent responsibility for the conditions and circumstances in your life. It requires a leap of faith to accept that you've molded and fashioned everything that's happened to you, both positive and unfavorable.

The good news is that the most critical learning lessons of life are hidden in unfavorable events. The wisdom we gain from them is in direct proportion to our willingness to take ownership of those events. It is this source of knowing that allows us to clearly separate what's important from those events that provide temporary ego enhancement.

> *The most critical learning lessons of life are hidden in unfavorable events. The wisdom we gain from them is in direct proportion to our willingness to take ownership of those events.*

As I shared above, creating quality and balance involves the resolution of a major unresolved situation. It is critical to work through these unresolved situations because, if ignored, they eventually turn into crises—mostly by our unconscious participation. Only after a breakthrough occurs, as in my realization regarding time with my daughters, will the how-to advice be of any use. Unless you recognize your power to create the desired change in your life, all the advice on the planet will be virtually useless!

> *Unless you recognize your power to create the desired change in your life, all the advice on the planet will be virtually useless!*

In order to acquire a quantitative sense of this fundamental principle—100% responsibility and 100% accountability—consider the implications of the diagram on page 43. I call it "The Responsibility Scale." This scale is based on the assumption that: Every individual has *available* 100% personal responsibility for the events that occur in his or her life.

Figure a. represents an individual who assumes he or she is, on average, 50% personally responsible and correspondingly 50% personally accountable for events in his or her life. This means that this individual abdicates, on average, 50% responsibility and correspondingly, he or she feels victimized and disempowered to influence those events.

Figure b. represents an individual who assumes 70% responsibility, on average, for the events that occur in his or her life. We can see how the *victim-disempowered* area is diminished relative to the responsible-accountable area.

Figure c. illustrates an individual whose predisposed assumption of personal responsibility is 90%. This mind-set is indicative of an individual who achieves, on average, most of his or her established goals in life.

The Responsibility Scale

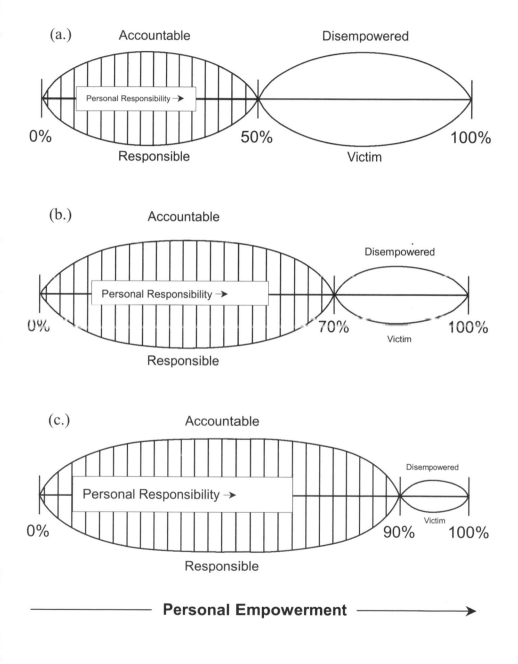

Notice the scale at the bottom of this figure has the phrase "Personal Empowerment." These three figures help us understand that the most important requirement for personal empowerment is the assumption of a high degree of personal responsibility and accountability. In essence, there is no such thing as a "highly empowered individual" who does not also claim a high degree of personal responsibility and accountability. The relationship between personal empowerment, personal responsibility, and personal accountability can be summarized by the following statement: *An individual is personally empowered only to the extent he or she assumes personal responsibility and accountability for what happens in his or her life.*

Now that you have a clear sense of ownership of what your life is like now, let's begin closing the gaps. It's time to begin taking action!

Chapter 4

Closing the Gaps –
Rewriting the Script of Your Life

*"Each second you can be reborn. Each second
there can be a new beginning. It is choice.
It is your choice."*

Clearwater

In chapter one I made brief mention of the basic building blocks of our life experience. Those building blocks are events and activities. The events and activities we experience determine the quality of our life.

When our activities are in alignment with our innermost values we often experience life quality. When they are not, we don't. Therefore the principle of life quality is simple. We change the quality of our life simply by changing activities and then fully experiencing those activities.

> *The principle of life quality is simple. We change the quality of our life simply by changing activities.*

Yes, changing activities does require determination and effort. And yes, the challenge of making changes ranges from simple to complex. In fact, sometimes it can be downright terrifying. But the principle still remains. You can instantly improve the quality of your life by looking for simple activity changes that will enhance the quality you experience.

> **You can instantly improve the quality of your life
> by looking for simple activity changes that will
> enhance the quality you experience.**

Here's one example. Let's assume you are in the habit of watching or listening to the news throughout the entire time you are getting ready in the morning. Each day the news is depressing and bad. Consequently, each morning you leave your house with negative feelings and a heavy heart. The activity that is putting you into this state is *watching the news*.

You've had enough! You resolve to improve your life quality by eliminating the activity that causes the negative feelings— watching the news—and replacing it with an activity that supports your value to be positive and upbeat. The activity you choose is *listening to music*. Now each morning, instead of watching the news, you listen to a favorite symphony, rock star, or jazz musician. Not only is the music exhilarating, the activity gives you a strong sense of satisfaction because it is driven by your desire to be positive and happy. Presto! Your life quality has improved and you leave your home with a positive attitude.

On the other end of the scale is the leap of faith made by Roben Grazadie when her mother became terminally ill.

> *Roben was at the height of her career when she learned her mother was terminally ill. Working as a consultant for a well-known business expert, she was also writing a book and speaking. She found herself having to make a choice between being potentially famous and extremely financially successful, and setting it all aside to be there for her mother.*
>
> *In her own words she said, "I made the choice from my heart. I thought of many people I'd worked with over the years who had sacrificed the things that were really important to them for big houses, cars, jets, and lots of money. They were some of the most miserable, unhappy*

people I'd ever met. They ended up with a lot of financial wealth but no emotional or spiritual wealth. I knew I had to honor what was in my heart or I would never be at peace and happy with myself." Roben left her position, sold her home, lived on her savings, and for eighteen months cared for her dying mother.

While on a three-day vacation with a friend she got a call from her father. Her mother had taken a turn for the worse and doctors said she would probably die within 12 hours. No matter how hard she tried to make it home in time, the trip would take at least a day and a half. She left immediately arriving home to her mother's side nearly 48 hours after the call. Amazingly, her mother was still alive. Roben went in, took her mother's hand and watched as she took her last breath.

"We bonded in a deep way during the year and a half I cared for her. I believe she was waiting and hanging on with every ounce of energy she had until I was in the room. I believe taking her last breath with me was her way of showing me honor and respect," says Roben.

When asked if fear was ever a factor in her decision she will tell you, "No, there was no fear in the choice to take care of Mom because I believed deep down inside that if I did the right thing God would take care of me."

Fear did become a factor, however, when she got back out into the world to look for work. She encountered a society that did not dominantly respect values like the ones that were the driving force behind her decision to put her career on hold and care for her mother. In fact, there were times when the doubts were huge. Interview after interview ended with each company being suspicious about how loyal and devoted she would be. After all, she had walked out on career success and fortune once before. What would stop her from doing it again? She felt frustrated and disheartened and filled with self-doubt. Feeling quite discouraged, she asked a close friend what good it had done her. His response was that it would prepare her better for service to society.

Roben told me that being able to share her story, believing that others may learn from her thought processes and her experience, has helped her recognize some of that service to society. Oh, and just so you don't worry, she is back on top pursuing her career goals and dreams.

This recounting of Roben's story hasn't even touched on the learning and the healing *she* experienced as she served her family and particularly her mother. You will find the account of that incredible journey in her book, *Seed in the Birdhouse – Sowing Seeds of Unconditional Love.*

By sharing only some of the details of what Roben went through I hope to clearly demonstrate the principle we discussed back in chapter three. The principles involved in identifying an innermost value and then having it challenged. Roben says she has no regrets. Given the same circumstances, she would make the same decision again.

Even though our innermost values are permanent and enduring over our lives, how we express them through our life activities can change. Such change is often provoked by learning and growing as a person. Some years ago, I used to be chairman of the department of chemistry at a fairly prestigious university. At the height of my career, I became passionately interested in personal growth. The more I learned about myself, the more I learned about the value of people and relationships.

My quest for experiential learning led me to other countries and the exploration of beliefs, values, and ways of living diametrically different from the U.S. I came to the conclusion there was more to life than simply publishing research papers and striving to become famous as a scientist—which is the direction I was headed. When I stopped to examine the inner passion of my life, it was simply to have those I could influence recognize the infinite potential within themselves for success and happiness.

So I chose to shift my venue of work from the university setting to the business world. In the business world, experiential learning is more accepted and embraced as key to exceptional performance. Within a week of my realization, I decided to rewrite the script of my life. I started a human resources consulting firm focused on personal and organizational transformation. I sometimes refer to my change in careers as a shift from "molecules to people."

The important point to recognize is that my innermost value that drives my new activity is unchanged. What has changed is the script or the activities that provide joy, satisfaction, and contribution to others.

A Holistic Approach

Remember earlier I told you there is only one rule in the new time paradigm, to see yourself as yourself, one complete whole individual, and live life with all your heart!

A holistic approach to work-life quality and balance begins with understanding that activities characterized by joy, passion, satisfaction, and love are sourced from innermost values. Therefore, clarifying what's important is where we begin if we want to put our fragmented self back together and rewrite the script of our life. This involves the in-depth exploration of activities that provide meaning, purpose, fulfillment, and peace of mind. In this case, in-depth exploration means going deeper inside ourselves than perhaps we've ever gone before.

Using the foregoing philosophy, here is a recipe for rewriting the script of your life.

1. Write a list of your innermost values and a corresponding activity, whether you are presently doing the activity or not.
2. Identify the most important activities in the areas of self, family, work, and service.

3. Evaluate the extent to which you fulfill each of these from a quality standpoint.

4. Resolve challenges and perceived consequences if you fully lived your most important activities.

5. Live the script of your life by integrating these activities into your 24-hour, 7-day work-life cycle.

Step 1: Write a List of Innermost Values and Activities

"Discover what drives you from within and
match it with real-world activities to give your
life new meaning."

Lynda Field
60 Ways to Change Your Life

The first three chapters of this book contain preparatory information for this step. We suggest you review your work-life balance surveys prior to this exercise. Use them to analyze gaps between your present state and your desired work-life condition.

The first step in rewriting the script of your life is writing a list of your innermost values and a corresponding activity for each. For example:

Innermost Value	Activity
Enjoy/protect nature	Hiking
Dignified elder care	Read to my Mother
Close family relationships	Time alone with each child
Meaningful work	Solving a client's problem
Love	A random act of kindness
Creativity	Developing new products/services
Teamwork	Work projects with others

Search diligently for innermost values that are not being openly expressed in activities you'd really like to be doing. At the same time, search for innermost values that drive activities you are currently doing; specifically those activities that are bringing you joy, satisfaction, meaning, and purpose.

As you proceed with this exercise, use every effort to go deeper inside yourself than you've ever gone before. Let your thoughts and ideas flow freely. Remember that innermost values are those that are enduring over your lifetime in the areas of self, family, work, and service. To assist you in this exercise we've provided examples of activities in each of these categories.

Self	Family
Those activities involving one's personal well-being – the balanced integration of body, mind, and spirit	Those activities involving significant personal relationships
• Hobbies • Gardening • Music • Personal centering • Creativity and innovation • Personal growth • Continuous learning • Reading • Support groups • Diet • Exercise • Time alone • Self introspection	• Child care • Elder care • Family events • Family activities • Quality time • Children's activities • Vacations • Family bonding • Marital harmony • Teaching • Family history • Travel • Meaningful conversations

Work	Service
Those activities primarily relating to earning a living or work life	Those activities involving contribution to others outside of work
<ul><li>Recognition/Reward</li><li>Teamwork</li><li>Establishing meaningful relationships</li><li>Professional development/growth</li><li>Career planning</li><li>Creativity</li><li>Continuous learning</li><li>Self-management</li><li>Employee support</li></ul>	<ul><li>Volunteerism</li><li>Youth activities</li><li>Community contributions</li><li>Religious activities</li><li>Being a good neighbor</li><li>Random acts of kindness</li><li>Political activities</li><li>Environmental protection</li><li>Financial contributions</li></ul>

Identify three to five innermost values in each category with a corresponding activity for each of the categories on the following pages.

List five innermost values and corresponding activities that involve your personal well-being—physically, mentally, and spiritually.

Self – Innermost Values	Corresponding Activities
1.	1.
2.	2.
3.	3.
4.	4.
5.	5.

List five innermost values and corresponding activities that involve your significant personal relationships.

Family – Innermost Values	Corresponding Activities
1.	1.
2.	2.
3.	3.
4.	4.
5.	5.

List five innermost values and corresponding activities that involve earning a living or your work life.

Work – Innermost Values	Corresponding Activities
1.	1.
2.	2.
3.	3.
4.	4.
5.	5.

List five innermost values and corresponding activities that involve your contribution to others.

Service – Innermost Values	Corresponding Activities
1.	1.
2.	2.
3.	3.
4.	4.
5.	5.

Step 2: Identify Your Most Important Activities

Life balance does not mean investing equal time in each category of your desired activities. It means investing time on activities in proportion to their worth, based upon your innermost values. In other words, *all activities are not created equal.* Not only that, they change over time! In the last exercise you identified some of your innermost values with their corresponding activities in four categories.

Let's take a minute here and use the story of the five balls, found in the novel, *Suzanne's Diary for Nicholas*, by author James Patterson, to reiterate that point.

> *The following day I had a coronary bypass at Mass General. It put me out of action for almost two months, and it was during my recuperation that I had time to think, really think, maybe for the first time in my life.*
>
> *I thoroughly examined my life in Boston, just how hectic it had become with rounds, overtime, and double shifts. I thought about how I'd been feeling just before this awful thing happened. I also dealt with my own denial. My family had a history of heart disease, and still I hadn't been as careful as I should have been.*
>
> *It was while I was recuperating that a friend told me the story of the five balls. Never forget this one, Nicky. This is terribly important.*

It goes like this:

Imagine life is a game in which you are juggling five balls. The balls are called work, family, health, friends, and integrity. And you're keeping all of them in the air. But one day you finally come to understand that work is a rubber ball. If you drop it, it will bounce back. The other four balls—family, health, friends, integrity—are made of glass. If you drop one of these, it will be irrevocably scuffed, nicked, perhaps even shattered. And once you truly understand the lesson of the five balls, you will have the beginnings of balance in your life.

Nicky, I finally understood.

The lesson of the five balls is clear. In the long run, not all innermost values and their corresponding activities have equal impact on the quality of our life. To avoid shattering or causing irrevocable damage to that which is most dear to us, we must carefully consider the short-term and long-term impact of our decisions. We can do this by projecting the impact of our decisions into a *probable future*.

Long-term values include family, self, and personal relationships. Short-term values include advancement, recognition and money.

As you complete step two by identifying your most important activities, think in terms of short-term and long-term impact. Complete this exercise while you are alone and free of distractions. Don't be rushed. Forget about what others might think if you did pursue some of those activities. Indulge yourself in the possibilities without worrying about the consequences at this point. Have fun! Dream! Imagine!

Step 3: Evaluate the Quality of Your Activities

What does it mean to evaluate these activities from a quality standpoint? We defined *life quality* as the sense of *satisfaction* we experience when we live congruent with our innermost values. When we are living those values we feel a sense of aliveness, joy, satisfaction, and meaning. If we have a need or desire to be doing activities important to us but we are not, we feel dissatisfied. How we feel then—satisfied or dissatisfied—is the basis for evaluating the extent to which you fulfill the activities in terms of quality.

I have been a diversity consultant for more than fifteen years. It is one of the most challenging activities (not jobs) I have ever attempted. Diversity tends to provoke some of the most in-depth beliefs, attitudes, and values we have about each other as people— some complementary, some not complementary. In spite of the resistance I experience from individuals and organizations to such exploration, we somehow always end the day on a positive note having learned how to appreciate each other more. Most of all, the participants discover "how *they* can make the greatest difference in their lives!" This is the essence of empowering others. This is my greatest joy in the so-called work that I do—to have others recognize the power within themselves to create the quality of life they desire.

As you reflect upon the activities you've listed on pages 53-56, use your emotional barometer. Place an "S" for satisfied, by those activities you are living to the extent you desire. Place a "D" for dissatisfied, by the activities you are not.

Step 4: Resolve Challenges and Perceived Consequences

"The ultimate measure of a person is not where he or she stands in moments of comfort and convenience, but where he or she stands in moments of challenge and adversity."

Dr. Martin Luther King, Jr.

You have created a list of innermost values with corresponding activities. You've identified the activities that are the most important to you and evaluated the extent to which you fulfill each of them. You are now on the threshold of making some decisions that will empower your work-life quality and balance. After all, it's your life to enjoy!

Standing on this threshold might feel a little like standing on the edge of a cliff experiencing acrophobia. You can undoubtedly make some minor adjustments immediately. This you can do by eliminating some counterproductive activities and replacing them with activities you really value.

On the other hand you realize if you really want to significantly change your work-life quality, it will require a major decision on your part. Perhaps, you are at a point where life circumstances have put you at a decision-making crossroads. Let me remind you, when you attempt to significantly change or make tough decisions about your work-life balance you will be faced with the greatest "perceived" threat to your security. This is your moment of truth.

Consider the dilemma faced by Bob and Rita.

> *Bob and Rita Colliedge are a working couple with two children, ages 5 and 3 years old. On the morning that Bob handles day care for their 3-year-old, his business team convenes a 7:00 a.m. Monday morning, emergency meeting. The meeting involves a new multimillion-dollar opportunity. Everyone is informed by e-mail, but Bob fails to check his e-mail on Sunday because of a family outing. He misses the meeting.*

Is Bob 100% responsible for missing the meeting? (Remember Chapter 3)

> *When Bob discovers he missed the meeting and was assigned a critical task that requires frequent travel over the next six months, he experiences stress and anxiety. The team leader informs Bob that he needs confirmation of Bob's assigned role on the team ASAP. He informs Bob how important this assignment can be to his career. Rita and Bob had agreed their careers were equally important. He promised Rita they would always discuss assignments that interfered with their balance of home and work responsibilities.*

> *When Bob approaches Rita he explains how important this six-month project could be to his career. In essence, it appears to be a "one-time" opportunity. He shares with her that his team leader suggested that the success of this multimillion-dollar project could result in a double promotion opportunity for him. Rita expresses concern that the project might lead to a trend in Bob's travel, and hence a deterioration of their relationship. She indicates that she is against him taking the assignment but will leave the final decision to him.*

If you identify mostly with Bob, would you take the assignment? How would you justify your answer?

If you identify mostly with Rita, how would you respond if Bob took the position? How would you justify your response?

What important innermost value is reflected by your decision?

Do you live consistent with this innermost value in difficult situations?

In the process of developing a career, we make crucial work-life decisions—sometimes without conscious awareness of their long-term consequences. Examples include:

- Extensive travel
- Working overtime
- Working at home
- Putting off the activities we value most
- Focusing on work while excluding family activities
- Neglecting one's spiritual, mental, and physical well-being

Taking responsibility for your life begins with discovering what's most important to you *in the short-term as well as the long run*—family, self, faith—and making a conscious choice between a short-term value (career aspirations) and a long-term value (family relationships) that comes from your inner self.

Second, it involves projecting that value and its activities into a *probable future*. What are the probable consequences to you personally and to your family relationships?

Third, ask yourself, "Is this probable future, with its consequences, acceptable to me?" Discuss your choice with family, an HR professional, and your manager. Then decide and go for it!

> *Bob and Rita – The real life solution*
>
> *Bob and Rita met for lunch to discuss Bob's situation, since it involved them both. They agreed that frequent travel, even in the short term, would be a dangerous precedent to set and would probably generate resentment from Rita, even if she pretended to go along with this particular assignment.*
>
> *They agreed to inform Bob's team leader that travel once a month over the six-month period for two days and one night would be acceptable. If not, he should find another role for Bob on the team.*

This incident provoked Bob and Rita to consciously define their life's careers and goals, based upon a balance of their individual and shared values. The joint decision made by Bob and Rita is a reflection of their commitment to each other that their personal relationship is more important than rapid career advancement.

It is also the recognition that upsetting their home-life responsibility balance could lead to the onset of interpersonal tension. Their joint decision is a reflection of their mutual alignment, respect, and commitment, and ultimately preservation of the quality of their interpersonal relationship.

In a nutshell…

- Your innermost values are those that define who you are when you are being honest within yourself and authentic in your relationships with others. They are tested most when difficult work-life choices must be made.

- Knowing your innermost personal values and how you prioritize them is the foundation for making difficult work-life balance decisions.

- Living true to your innermost values requires personal responsibility and personal accountability for the events that occur in your life. Personal responsibility is the willingness to be the principal source of what happens in your life.

- The more you accept personal responsibility, the more you determine what happens in your life. Personal accountability is the willingness to own the results that occur in your life.

- If you own the results—whether fair or unfair—you have the power to initiate proactive solutions. If not, then it's necessary for someone else to take action on your behalf, which may or may not happen.

As you experience your personal moments of truth you may be thinking you are indispensable. This mind-set usually leads to stress and a feeling of overwhelm. Most people who are constantly overwhelmed are:

- Attempting to do too much
- Not delegating
- Procrastinating
- Allowing too many interruptions
- Not good at life management
- Into their ego

What all these points have in common is a sense of self-importance. They indicate a mind-set of "Nobody can do it as well as I can." Often, individuals in this state really do live in the illusion that they are indispensable. Others see them as "struggling with the need to be in control."

To change your life you'll need to get over yourself. I know this is true and I know you can. For most of my business career I was guilty of all of the above. Consequently, I worked all the time. On ski trips I'd be doing work at a table in the condo while my friends would be enjoying each other's company. On vacations to Hawaii, I'd do the same thing. I'd sit on the beach and work while my friends were swimming and surfing.

Perhaps the most negative impact of my work style was this: I did not do a good job of growing the people around me. In short, the mind-set of "I'm indispensable" has no redeeming quality for the practitioner, the family, or the business. It's a barrier to achieving work-life quality and balance.

If this sounds like you, begin with a shift in mind-set. Look around and get in touch with reality. Get over yourself. Nobody is indispensable. Make the appropriate adjustments that apply to you and trust that most things have a way of working out when you let others assume accountability for their own responsibilities. Don't carry such a big workload that there is no room for life balance.

Step 5: Integrate Your Chosen Activities into Your 24-hour, 7-day Work-Life Cycle

The activities you desire to execute that are consistent with your innermost values are *vital* to the achievement of your work-life quality and balance. *Vital* events are concerned with, or necessary to, the maintenance of life. Unfortunately those are often the activities that become subordinated to less important and even trivial activities. This happens when one is not skillful at choosing and managing daily activities. The formula for integrating *vital* activities into your 24-hour, 7-day work-life cycle can be found in the next two chapters.

Chapter 5

Lights! Camera! Action! –
Living the Script of Your Life

It was a tough hard working business week in Chicago. Friday's work finally came to a close. I hailed a cab and headed for the Chicago O'Hare airport. I was exhausted. The driver made a wrong turn and got us stuck in a traffic jam. I became irritated and stressed.

I couldn't wait to get to the airport, catch United Airlines Flight 729, and get more work done on the airplane. After all, that's what out-of-balance workaholics do. To me it was just another flight taking me home. I had no idea that flight would change my life dramatically.

Finally, I was seated on the plane in the very last row. Hissing air and groaning hydraulic systems signaled the plane was coming to life. Then came the familiar announcement, "Please give us your attention during the safety instructions." I fly so much, most of the time I don't even bother to look up, but this time I did. That's when my life changed forever.

There she was, one of two flight attendants working the back cabin. By the time the oxygen demonstration was over, I was the one who needed oxygen. She took my breath away! And what subsequently ensued is the fairytale romance movies are made of. Amidst sunsets and rising heat waves on the tarmac, we kissed and said our longing goodbyes.

On our third date we planned our honeymoon. The fourth date we were engaged, and we got married very quickly after that. Then...the honeymoon was over! We had fallen in love with each other's strengths and had gone home to live with our differences. But love is blind! I thought she was perfect!

We discovered we are different in every conceivable way. One day a friend of mine said, "I don't want to make you feel bad, but did you ever notice Brenda has no eyelashes?"

I said, "No, I never noticed." But what he said bugged me, so I went home to take a closer look. Well, the truth is, Brenda has eyelashes, but very few…hmmmm. After that, I wanted eyelashes! So I fixed the problem! I bought her a pair! And that was the beginning of me trying to *fix* my spouse. At the time, I didn't realize how futile and unkind it was.

I was somewhat of an obsessive-compulsive workaholic. I believed there was only one way to do things—MY WAY! Everything had to be straight at all times. No clutter! Once the plan was set, that was it! Don't deviate! No forgiveness for not being perfect. No time for fun. Keep moving! Start working early in the morning and don't let up. Not even time for a good lunch.

After several years of me *coaching* Brenda on how to do things properly, my marriage seemed to be going flat. One day I said, "You're not the same person I married."

She said, "You know why, don't you?" I asked why.

"I've become just like you! That's what you wanted, isn't it?"

OUCH! It was a stinging comment. Clearly I had missed unlimited opportunities in the years past for a fuller, richer life and a better marriage.

I was ready to learn. I wanted the life skills that came with Brenda innately. She knew how to savor life's experiences and I did not. A friend of mine once said, "Brenda is magical." He was right. That's why Flight 729 changed my life. I wanted the magic again. I wanted to make up for lost time. I even went out and bought her a new wedding band with the inscription "Catching Up!" engraved on the inside.

I am living proof that life quality skills can be learned. There are six critical ones to begin with. Others will come but you must first learn to:

- Be where you are
- Allow spontaneity
- Discover the joys of curiosity
- Integrate, don't contaminate, work-life activities
- Plan, simplify, and be strong

- Chip away, every day!

Each of these will be discussed on the following pages.

Be Where You Are

This is the skill of allowing yourself to fully experience an activity. It is the ability to live in the moment. It is savoring an activity by concentrating your entire life force on the moment.

For example, my wife can extract more pleasure from sipping a Coca Cola than you can imagine. There is more going on with the beverage than most of us realize. She notices the light coming through the caramel color and the sparkling ice cubes. She is enchanted with the bubbles dancing to the surface. She anticipates the first sip, the sting on the end of her tongue and gives her attention to the taste and how it feels as she swallows. Sound extreme? Maybe, but nobody gets more value from a simple soft drink than she does.

Sometimes, this skill is also called "being in the moment." It's when you give your undivided attention to something or someone. When I used to go to restaurants, I would order my main course when a waiter or waitress came to ask what I would like to drink. The idea was to minimize the time away from work and increase the efficiency of dining. My mind was somewhere in the future on what I needed to do or accomplish. Then, one luncheon, my wife said, "Put those thoughts away!" I said, "What?" My first thought was, "I can't exist without them!" My second thought was, "She is truly beautiful!" From that moment throughout lunch, she had my undivided attention. That experience began a process of my learning how to be more *present* in whatever I might be doing.

What about you? When was the last time you savored a simple soft drink? And what about dinner? Do you dine or just eat? Do you taste your food or gulp it down? The dinner table is a good place to start practicing the life skill of being where you are. Then expand the skill to all of your activities. It will enrich the quality of your life.

On a scale of 1 to 10, how often do you practice the life skill of being where you are?

1	2	3	4	5	6	7	8	9	10

I don't know where I am   Sometimes I can be found in the moment   I am focused in the moment

Allow Spontaneity

Spontaneity enriches any activity that otherwise might be more mundane. I learned this from a fellow speaker friend of mine in a very simple way. He was coaching me on the skill. He said, "Open your Day-Timer® at random and put a red dot on a future page. Then close it and forget about it. When that day finally arrives and you see the red dot, do something unexpected for somebody. For example, send some flowers for no reason at all. You'll find the activity is far more joyous and impactful than when the flowers are expected."

Random, planned spontaneity like I described above is a good way to begin if you don't come by it naturally. To most people the very idea of *planned spontaneity* is an oxymoron. But to those of us who are not spontaneous, it is a method or a technique for learning to be spontaneous. For me, it has been a very tough skill to master. I'm still not as good as I'd like to be but I am a lot more spontaneous today than I was even a year ago. I suppose much of it started with the movie incident. It's been a long time since then but—

It was nearly 9:00 p.m. I was sitting upstairs in our home, kind of bored, and it was too early to go to bed. Suddenly the doorbell rang. Two friends burst through the front door shouting "Hey, let's go to a movie! It starts in five minutes." My spouse, of course, shot out the front door not even having to think about it. What did I do? I didn't go. I always enjoyed being around those friends and there wasn't a single reason why I couldn't go. It was just *too* spontaneous for me.

As usual, some inexplicable fear prevented me from doing something on the spur of the moment. The barrier kept me from taking side trips while on vacation, too. Even worse, I was often not flexible enough to stop working long enough to listen, really listen, to one of my children when they interrupted me. Those of us who aren't spontaneous miss countless moments of joy because we suffer from the need to have "controlled planning." Too busy to seize a moment that might never occur again.

More recently, I've learned to use my intuition as an impetus for *acts of spontaneity*. For example, when I feel good about a friend, I send him or her a card, gift, or extend an invitation to lunch. When the thought hits me that an employee has performed exceptionally over a period of months, I spontaneously ask my intuition, "how should I reward or acknowledge that person?" The answer is often a bonus, a day off, a frequent flyer trip on my miles, or whatever comes to me. My intuition rarely, if ever, fails me.

On a scale of 1–10 how often do you allow yourself to practice the life skill of spontaneity?

1	2	3	4	5	6	7	8	9	10
I am rarely spontaneous				Sometimes I'm spontaneous				I am often spontaneous	

Discover the Joys of Curiosity

I remember the day I was reminded about the joys of curiosity. I was hiking with my best friend. We hit the trail early in the morning. That's the best time to smell nature's perfume and feel the gentle warmth of the sun's morning rays. We had a great hike. On our return in the early afternoon, as we rounded the last bend, I could see the canyon road and my parked car. I glanced at my watch and noticed it was 2:00 p.m. The exact time I planned to finish my hike. I felt a rush of pride about my ability to manage my time and always do everything on a schedule.

As we reached the road, my friend glanced toward the creek. There sitting on the edge of the water was a mutual friend— Ardean Watts, the director of music at our local university. We shouted, "Hey, Ardean! What are ya doin'?"

He motioned for us to come over. "Look," he said. "Get down here really close. See? I'm watching a spider spin its web."

I was taken aback and a little bit envious. I couldn't remember the last time I watched a spider spinning its web but I know I was a child. How about you? I resolved to lighten up on my scheduled tunnel-vision life and re-learn childlike curiosity again. Fortunately, I have two young daughters who insistently ask questions about practically everything they experience. Instead of becoming impatient, as I used to, I find myself re-learning the curiosity I set aside as an adolescent.

Curiosity, like spontaneity, can lace our life with microbursts of joy. It's a natural skill we all had when we were children. We can practice the skill anytime, anyplace. Curiosity keeps us plugged into life.

On a scale of 1–10, how often do you practice the life skill of curiosity?

1	2	3	4	5	6	7	8	9	10
I am rarely curious				Sometimes I'm curious				I am often curious	

Integrate, Don't Contaminate, Work-Life Activities

Now that our society operates on a 24-hour, 7-day work-life cycle it is important to distinguish between the integration of work-life and the contamination of work-life. Work-life integration is the *alternate* execution of work and personal life activities in a manner that permits us to fully experience the quality of both. Work-life contamination is the *simultaneous* execution of work and personal life activities in a manner that prevents us from fully experiencing the quality of either.

Cell phones, when not used skillfully, contaminate work and personal life activities. I was recently hiking in the Wasatch Mountains in an area that has 28 varieties of wildflowers. It was a beautiful morning and the flowers were at their peak. As I was walking down the trail I saw a man and his female companion coming up. I first observed them at quite a distance but I could hear a loud conversation.

I continued to stop about every ten yards to drink in the scenery and marvel at the colors, the shadows, and the variety of flowers carpeting the mountainside. That loud conversation just kept coming up the trail destroying the serenity of the moment. Straight up the trail he came, not looking to the left or right, and not giving any attention to his companion. I realized he was talking on his cell phone. He missed most of the scenery and probably a lot more.

Why go for a hike if you aren't going to be present? What is so critical about work that it has to be accomplished under such circumstances? Sure urgencies occur, but some of us operate this way continuously. This is work-life contamination. Work-life integration would be to fully experience the quality of both activities by executing them at different times. For example, making the call at the beginning of the trailhead or the end of the hike.

A down-to-earth example of this phenomenon is using a cell phone while having a meal with someone. I frequently observe the other person sitting there while their companion carries on an involved conversation with someone else. I've often wondered how the companion must feel. Imagine having lunch with someone and his or her friend walks up to the table. The two carry on an animated, five-minute conversation while ignoring you. How would *you* feel?

Time management experts refer to doing more than one activity at a time as multi-tasking. In today's fast-paced world it is hard to avoid it but there is definitely an appropriate way to do it. Multi-tasking works best when the activities being combined naturally hitchhike one to the other; are physical in nature; don't require a lot of thought; and when another human isn't involved.

Examples of work-life contamination are:

- Opening your mail while carrying on an important business conversation with somebody in your office.

- Working on your computer while watching a child's soccer game.
- Attending a seminar and bringing your business work to read or work on.

On a scale of 1–10, how often do you practice the life skill of work-life integration?

1	2	3	4	5	6	7	8	9	10
I usually contaminate				Sometimes I integrate			I integrate most of the time		

Plan, Simplify, and Be Strong!

One of my long-time friends who has been very successful taught me the "Richards Principle," named for his father who practiced it throughout his life. On numerous occasions over the years, as we faced challenges, he quoted the principle to me. It goes like this: Plan, simplify, and be strong!

This principle is good advice for anybody who wants a higher quality of life. Consider the impact of these three powerful keys:

Plan – By rewriting the script of your life you have created your plan. You may still need to work out some of the details but the new script provides guidelines to follow. I've learned that the first, most important step in achieving anything is knowing what you want and then figuring out how to get there. When I can visualize what I want with such clarity that I can see, feel, and even taste it, I can describe the exact conditions of its accomplishment. I do this activity at the beginning of every new year.

Simplify – Identifying your innermost values is one of the best ways to bring to your awareness attitudes and activities that complicate and clutter your life. Eliminating activities that are not connected to innermost values will simplify your life in ways you haven't even imagined. Remember, the activities of your plan should bring joy, happiness, and satisfaction *during the trip*, not just at reaching your destination.

Be Strong – It is essential to practice both mental and physical toughness. If you are not strong about following your script you will end up following one written by somebody else. However, being strong about a script presupposes you have one! If you don't, you might create one.

On a scale of 1–10, how often do you practice the life skill of plan, simplify, and be strong?

1	2	3	4	5	6	7	8	9	10
Not my script				Sometimes my script			My script is simple and I'm strong!		

Did you notice that I asked you how often you *practice* each of the five preceding life skills? I chose the word *practice* for a reason. I could have asked you, "How good are you at this life skill," but I know from experience that it takes *practice*. Yes, some people come by it naturally but most of us have to work at it. Remember, I speak from experience. I've already confessed to my own reformation. The story in the following section explains what I mean.

Chip Away, Every Day!

Many years ago after my father built his first home he decided he wanted a stone wall in his backyard. This was to be a backdrop for his garden. We are talking stone masonry. This means starting with sandstone in big chunks. Then individually with a hammer and chisel, cutting every stone out by hand. Nothing is pre-cut. Even in those days the price was prohibitive. It is labor intensive. But my dad wanted the wall. He asked a stonemason to give him some tips. People are nice, and he did. After that, dad built a cutting platform in the back yard, whacked away on a few stones, and said to himself, "I can do this."

From that point forward, every morning almost without exception, my dad was out in what he called "the rock pile" banging on stone. These were some of the most embarrassing moments of my childhood. It was noisy and everybody knew it was my dad.

I remember the middle of the winter hearing the noise at 5:00 a.m. I parted the drapes and looked into the backyard. It was dark out there and snowing lightly. There was one electric light bulb rigged up casting an eerie light on the snow. There was dad, all bundled up in a big parka, banging on stone. To me, it seemed bizarre.

One morning at 5:00 a.m. our next-door neighbor, Oliver Richards, couldn't stand the racket any longer. His second-floor bedroom overlooked the rock pile. It was the noisiest place in the neighborhood. He was furious. He flew out of bed, rushed to the window, and standing in his pajamas, shouted down at my dad, "Hey Bill! What's wrong with you? Can't you sleep down there?"

My father, who is a very funny man, shouted back, "Are you kidding me? Not with all this noise going on!" And he just kept banging and chipping away. There was friction between these two guys that went on for five years.

At the end of five years the wall was finished and it was time to enjoy his work. Dad pulled up a chaise lounge, poured a drink, looked at the wall and became troubled. His skill in stone masonry had improved so much over the five-year period, it looked as though the first third of the wall had been built by a different stonemason. With practice, day after day, week after week, month after month, and year after year he'd gotten better and better. His progress was so obvious he couldn't stand it. Sure enough, one day he started tearing down the first third of the wall. All of those stones were hauled away. New stones were brought in and the process began again.

Midway through the second attempt he was stricken with polio and became paralyzed. He couldn't turn over in bed without the assistance of family members. He fought his way back from the disease and got back on the rock pile. Finally the wall was finished. It was an eight-year project.

Shortly after that, somebody climbed on an airplane, flew into our town and photographed the wall. That wall became the feature article of a major garden magazine. It got a four-page spread.

My father passed away at the age of ninety-two. I was visiting with him shortly before his death. I said, "You know what, Dad? I frequently tell people in my seminars about your wall."

He brightened up a little and said, "Let me tell you about my wall. Next time you are over at the house look at it closely. You won't find a hairline crack anywhere and I'll tell you why. I built that wall on a foundation of five tons of concrete all mixed by hand in a wheelbarrow." The wall is a magnificent thing. It has always been the spot for family gatherings.

But what does my dad's wall have to do with our subject of work-life balance? I'll explain. Creating work-life balance is like building the wall because you must first start with a foundation. The work-life balance foundation is innermost values. Once you have identified your innermost values you must then go to the *rock pile,* or in this case, the *activity pile,* every day and begin to chip away relentlessly on those activities that correspond to your values.

My father used a hammer and chisel to shape each stone. In the next chapter you will find day-to-day tools to help you choose and mold each activity you use to build value and meaning into your life. And remember, you will improve each of these skills as you *practice* them day after day, week after week, and month after month.

Chapter 6

One Day at a Time –
Directing Your Daily Activity Traffic

*"Concentration of power is the ability to focus upon
and accomplish the most vital priorities."*

Charles R. Hobbs, Ph.D.

We began the book by contemplating our lifeline to discover the answer to the question, "What's really important to me?" When we are clear about the answer to that question, it provides the basis for the more focused question, "What's important *today*?" After all, our lifeline is really just a series of day-lines connected together. At some point, each of us comes to the realization that our lives are the cumulative result of the day-to-day choices we've made; and that we live and die with our choices.

> *At some point each of us comes to the realization
> that our lives are the cumulative result of the
> day-to-day choices we've made; and that we
> live and die with our choices.*

For this reason the most critical skill in managing each day, and ultimately our life, is the skill of choosing. There will never be time to do everything, but there will always be time to do the most *vital* activities—the ones you choose to help you enrich your life and excel at your work.

We each have only three *primary* resources available to us: time, life energy, and the ability to choose. These three resources are fundamental because, without exception, they are available to every individual. Each of us is given the same number of hours in a day. Each of us has our own personal energy. And each of us has the power to choose how we will use those hours and our energy.

79

The truth is, there are only two ways we can use our time and energy. We can invest them by putting them to profitable use, or we can waste them! Investing our personal resources, our time, our energy, and our power to choose, is very much like investing money. When we invest our money wisely, we enrich our bank accounts. Similarly, when we invest ourselves wisely, we enrich the quality of our lives.

> *When we invest our money wisely, we enrich our bank accounts. When we invest ourselves wisely, we enrich the quality of our lives.*

Taking the investment principle one step further we recognize that money invested wisely yields interest or more money. In the same way, our personal energy invested wisely on *vital* activities yields benefits too! These benefits accrue in a variety of areas depending on where our investment is made.

Personal investment dividends can enrich our lives intellectually, physically, emotionally, spiritually, and financially. They can have a profound and lasting effect on our family and our community. How can we possibly put a dollar value on these things? Truly, the greatest worth of our personal investment is not measured by financial gain but rather in the things money cannot buy.

So, the answer to the smaller but very important question "What's important *today*?" or "What is *vital today*?" is a matter of *choosing* those activities that yield the highest life quality return on your investment and *avoiding* those that have little or no return.

Next to your life energy in importance is the power you have to *choose* how you spend that life energy. When all is said and done, the quality and balance in your life lies in the choices you make each day.

> **When all is said and done, the quality and balance in your life lies in the choices you make each day.**

Knowing which activities to *choose* and which activities to *avoid* gets easier as you learn to identify your ***vital*** activities and focus your energy on them. Understanding what's really ***vital*** brings purpose to each day. Purpose is an energy source. The daily activities we accomplish with our energy become visible statements of our commitment.

> **Understanding what's really vital brings purpose to each day. Purpose is an energy source.**

In the new time paradigm there is one principle that is essential for getting the best return on our investment of time and personal resources. That principle is *concentration of power.*

Concentration of power is the ability to focus upon and accomplish the most vital priorities. A priority is an activity to which we assign a value. Vital priorities are high payoff and crucial. In business, vital priorities are essential for the existence, continuation, and well-being of the organization. In our personal life they are the priorities that align with our innermost values.

> **In business, vital priorities are essential for the existence, continuation, and well-being of the organization. In our personal life they are the priorities that align with our innermost values.**

The first step toward achieving concentration of power is to develop the ability to quickly categorize activities according to how vital and urgent they are. It helps to distinguish priorities from urgencies.

Urgencies are situations or conditions that require some immediate action on our part. In some cases it might be inaction.

81

Nevertheless, when an *urgency* occurs, we must respond. Urgencies are created in a variety of ways. You've experienced most of them: a sudden demand from the boss; a time-sensitive opportunity; an accident; a close deadline; a request from a friend; certain e-mails and voice messages; a drop-in visitor; or a sick child. The list goes on and on. In the new paradigm, urgencies have increased in frequency and complexity. We must be able to edit urgencies as they pop up throughout the day.

Once we understand the difference between priorities and urgencies we are in a better position to *choose and avoid*. All activities can quickly be categorized according to how vital and urgent they are, as illustrated by the diagram on the following page.

We assigned the colors of the traffic light to the four kinds of activities with which we deal—Red, Green, Yellow, and Gray. (Okay, there isn't really a gray light but use your imagination. We promise, it will make perfect sense.)

Know when to STOP! Know when to GO! When to use CAUTION! And when to say NO!

We can use a familiar symbol, the traffic light, to help us remember the four types of activities and the actions to take when we face them, as shown below.

Know when to STOP! Know when to GO!
When to use CAUTION!
And when to say NO!

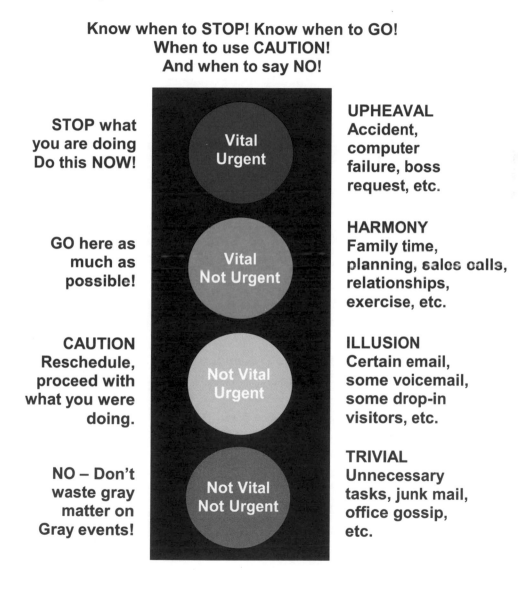

STOP what you are doing Do this NOW!

Vital Urgent

UPHEAVAL Accident, computer failure, boss request, etc.

GO here as much as possible!

Vital Not Urgent

HARMONY Family time, planning, sales calls, relationships, exercise, etc.

CAUTION Reschedule, proceed with what you were doing.

Not Vital Urgent

ILLUSION Certain email, some voicemail, some drop-in visitors, etc.

NO – Don't waste gray matter on Gray events!

Not Vital Not Urgent

TRIVIAL Unnecessary tasks, junk mail, office gossip, etc.

Know When to STOP!

Red activities are both vital and urgent. When facing a Red activity STOP whatever else you are doing and address the Red activity NOW! As Red activities pop up during the day, they aren't hard to recognize. Just ask my brother Paul. Paul is in his late fifties. He's a handsome man with a bit of gray hair around his temples. He dresses impeccably and works in a jewelry store. Upon entering his store one is overcome with a feeling of elegance.

On this particular day he was showing an exquisite diamond to a young couple shopping for an engagement ring. He had the diamond up under a light in a pair of tweezers as he expounded about color, clarity, and cut. He was really "romancing that stone!" Noticing a speck of dust, he inhaled to blow it off the diamond. Just then the tweezers snapped, shooting the diamond like a bullet into the back of his throat. He gagged and swallowed a $9,000 dollar diamond in front of his customers. It was vital and it was urgent!! Five days later the diamond was retrieved. Five days of "diamond in the rough." In a newspaper article about the incident, the last line stated, "The customers decided to purchase another stone."

Red activities often catch us off guard, but when they occur we know we must take action. Red activities put us in a state of upheaval and plans are put on hold in order to address such unexpected events. Some examples, other than swallowing a diamond, are: the computer system is down; a customer has just asked for a proposal and they want it now; your child fell off the monkey bars at school and needs to be taken to the hospital for stitches; an immediate request from your manager; a customer changes a scheduled presentation the day before the meeting; etc! These kinds of activities are no-brainer decisions. They occur, we respond.

Take a moment now and identify three to five Red activities that could occur in your workplace and/or personal life. Make sure they are both *urgent* and *vital*. The activities you list must qualify for your immediate attention. (Remember, this book is to be used for writing, scribbling, doodling, drawing, and whatever else *you* choose!)

1.

2.

3.

4.

5.

Know When to GO!

Green activities are vital but not urgent. Green means: GO there as much as possible. Green reminds us that these activities are value-added in our work-life. They are necessary for the existence and continuation of the business. On a personal basis, Green activities are the ones that bring quality and balance to our life. It is through Green activities that we build and maintain strong relationships, serve others, and improve ourselves. When doing these activities that are vital, but not urgent, we are typically in a state of composure, alignment, and harmony.

Green activities will often haunt us later if we procrastinate addressing them. I was reminded of that when my son, a college student, lamented the fact that I was too busy to read to him as a child. Yes, a Green activity can be as simple and crucial as that. All activities that are tied to our innermost values are Green activities including those that seem small or mundane, and those that are fun and recreational. Green activities include: long-range planning, exercise, relationship building, sales calls, family time, etc.

Take a moment and identify three to five Green activities that are crucial to the success of your business and quality of life.

1.

2.

3.

4.

5.

When to Use CAUTION!

It isn't easy being Green. One reason is that Red and Yellow activities are so challenging. Yellow activities are urgent but not vital. Yellow activities create an illusion of the need for immediate action. When we succumb to the temptation to handle these activities as they occur, we are operating in a state of *delusion*. When we resist the temptation to respond *now* our plans proceed as scheduled and these activities are rescheduled so they can be addressed at a more appropriate time in the future.

The color yellow reminds us to use caution. For example, you are preparing for an imminent conference call just as a co-worker shows up for a chat. It's urgent because the co-worker is there and you must respond. At the same time, the activity being brought to you is far from vital. And so it goes with some visitors, some telephone calls, some e-mail, and some voice mail. *Caution!* These kinds of urgencies can interfere with your concentration of power. The consummate self-manager knows what to *choose* and what to *refuse* and has the fortitude to say "No! Not now!"

Take a moment and identify three to five typical Yellow events that you commonly experience which should be rescheduled to be accomplished at a later time.

1.

2.

3.

4.

5.

And When to Say NO!

The fourth type of activity is gray—gray means RETHINK THIS ACTIVITY! Gray activities are not urgent and they are not vital. These are activities, behaviors, and practices that are of little or no value to self and others. When involved with these activities, we are primarily engaged in *trivia*.

These types of activities become an escape for those of us who aren't coping constructively with our daily activities. For example, a recent study reveals that the average American employee spends 30 minutes a day surfing the Internet on company time. Another example is opening junk mail when you know you are going to throw it in the recycle bin anyway. Some Gray activities are not only trivial, they can be destructive, such as countless hours spent on office gossip, reading junk mail, unnecessary tasks, etc. Avoid wasting gray matter on Gray events! In order to avoid both Yellow and/or Gray activities, one of our employees does a daily log of her Green activities. Then she evaluates how much these have been dominant during the day and makes appropriate adjustments.

Take a moment and identify three to five Gray activities that could involve you or a co-worker in the workplace.

1.

2.

3.

4.

5.

So how do you operate? Where do you spend your hours and energy? What is the state in which you are operating most of the time? Is it harmony (green), upheaval (red), illusion (yellow) or trivia (gray)?

You may be thinking to yourself that the concepts illustrated by the traffic light seem awfully familiar. And in fact, they are. Charles R. Hobbs, Ph.D., introduced me to the process of categorizing events based upon how vital and urgent they are when I worked for him promoting his Time Power® system. This information is found in his book *Time Power*, published by Harper & Row in 1988. And in fact, these concepts are so powerful they have been included in some form or another by many different time management programs over the years. Charles sold his seminar copyrights to Day-Timers® Inc. As Day-Timers' authorized training partner, I have included portions of this material with permission.

By attaching the use of *vital* and *urgent* to something as common as the traffic light you can quickly categorize an activity and easily remember how to proceed. Let's apply these tools to how we manage our lives in the next chapter.

Chapter 7

Getting Down to Business –
Tools for Life Management

"The people who get on in this world are the people
who get up and look for the circumstances they
want, and if they can't find them, make them."

George Bernard Shaw

Tracking Your Energy Investments

Many of us don't really know where our time and energy go because it's impossible to mentally track our activities. Imagine trying to manage money without a check register. Trying to track all of our financial transactions in our mind without records would be very frustrating, if not impossible. It is even more difficult to track our investment of energy and the activities upon which it is committed.

If we are to perform in the workplace at the levels required today, while balancing our lives, we must focus our energy on carefully selected activities. Tracking our activities for just one week is an eye-opening experience. It helps us recognize habits and trends. It will reveal to us how we might change our method of operating to achieve better concentration of power.

> *Tracking our activities for just one week is an*
> *eye-opening experience. It helps us recognize*
> *habits and trends.*

Activities can easily be tracked using the Work/Life Activity Record. This tool is unique in its simplicity. It's much easier to use than a traditional time log where, to get an accurate picture, you must remind yourself to stop every 15-20 minutes and record your activities. With the Work/Life Activity Record, shown on page 92, you log your activities only when you have completed one activity and you are ready to begin another.

In the left-hand column, the *time-of-day* is listed by hours with space to indicate specific periods during the hour. Next to that there is space to describe the activity followed by four columns, each representing the type of activity—Red, Green, Yellow, or Gray.

Put a mark next to the time you begin the first activity of the day. Do not write in the description until you have completed it and you are ready to move on to the next one. As you transition from one activity to the next, simply put another mark on the line next to the time you completed the activity and, in the space provided, describe in a word or two what the activity was. Then record the number of periods (10 minute intervals) of time it took in the column corresponding to the type of event it was—Red, Green, Yellow, or Gray. At the end of the day you'll have an accurate history of which type of activities consumed your time and energy throughout the day.

WORK/LIFE ACTIVITY RECORD

*"Where does your time go?"*SM

Date: _____

Time	Event / Activity	R	G	Y	GY
7:00					
7:10					
7:20					
7:30					
7:40					
7:50					
8:00					
8:10					
8:20					
8:30					
8:40					
8:50					
9:00					
9:10					
9:20					
9:30					
9:40					
9:50					
10:00					
10:10					
10:20					
10:30					
10:40					
10:50					
11:00					
11:10					
11:20					
11:30					
11:40					
11:50					
12:00					
12:10					
12:20					
12:30					
12:40					
12:50					
1:00					
1:10					
1:20					
1:30					
1:40					
1:50					

RED –Vital / Urgent – Stop what you're doing - do this NOW!

GREEN –Vital / Not urgent - Quality of Life / Where the money is!

YELLOW –Not vital / Urgent –Caution, may be a waste of time. re-evaluate!

GRAY –Not vital / Not urgent – Don't waste gray matter on gray events!

2:00				
2:10				
2:20				
2:30				
2:40				
2:50				
3:00				
3:10				
3:20				
3:30				
3:40				
3:50				
4:00				
4:10				
4:20				
4:30				
4:40				
4:50				
5:00				
5:10				
5:20				
5:30				
5:40				
5:50				
6:00				
6:10				
6:20				
6:30				
6:40				
6:50				
7:00				
7:10				
7:20				
7:30				
7:40				
7:50				
8:00				
8:10				
8:20				
8:30				
8:40				
8:50				
9:00				
9:10				
9:20				
9:30				
9:40				
9:50				
10:00				
Totals				

©TW2001

CANNONWOOD
High Performance Seminars
(801) 277-6500

Innovations International
(801) 268-3313

91

The following guidelines will help you maximize use of the activity record:

- Carry the activity record with you everywhere you go and fill it out as soon as you complete an activity.
- Be completely honest with yourself—making up details to make yourself look good on paper won't serve your purpose.
- Do not omit details. List interruptions and assign them a color, too.
- Do not rely on your memory. Mark the activity record at the completion of every activity. It takes a little getting used to but you'll be amazed at how valuable this little tool will become. The motivation it can provide is worth the effort.
- Use the activity record to improve your choices. Plan to do a thorough analysis of your day to help you improve tomorrow's choices.

At the end of the day, total the time periods spent on each color. Obviously, a predominantly *green* day is ideal. Green means you focused on the activities that make money and promote life quality.

What percentage of your day was spent doing Green (vital – not urgent) activities?

What percentage of your day was spent doing Red (vital – urgent) activities? Take a minute and analyze your Red activities. Are any of them Green activities that you just plain waited too long to get around to? Some Red activities are truly legitimate. Many can be completely avoided by focusing consistently on Green activities.

What percentage of your day was spent doing Yellow activities? Did you recognize them and reschedule them for a more appropriate time?

What percentage of your day did you waste gray matter on Gray activities? What are your plans to eliminate Gray activities from your daily traffic?

Consider this next idea carefully. If you focused an extra hour per day on Green activities and you did that for one year, you would have refocused more than six, forty-hour work-weeks. Now carefully consider what a powerful impact this would have on your personal work-life balance. In planning tomorrow's activities, seriously study and find creative ways you can rearrange and reschedule activities to achieve an extra hour a day involved in Green activities.

Gaining this concentration and focus in the midst of our very fast-paced, chaotic world begins with awareness. Yes, being aware in the midst of chaos can be a challenge but it is an essential step in moving toward more effective self-management and it can be done. Let me say that again—IT CAN BE DONE. There really is hope. Gaining more control over your day is a matter of self-management. And self-management is the ability to effectively choose and perform those daily activities that create:

- Personal and professional value to you
- High performance and organizational success

The Real Value of the Activity Record

Continuous use of the Work/Life Activity Record will improve your ability to *choose* activities, *arrange* activities, *focus* on the most *vital* activities, and ultimately *accomplish* activities. Managing yourself through a day in the workplace requires these four essential skills.

The utilization of these skills requires self-discipline, intuition, and even courage—the discipline to do what you don't want to do; the intuition to know when to be flexible; and the courage to say "no" to intrusive events.

> *The ability to choose, arrange, focus, and accomplish your most vital activities requires self-discipline, intuition, and courage.*

The truth is—overcoming personal inertia and generating high performance during a chaotic day is not easy for most of us. Perhaps that's why we call it work! Determining our skill level in these areas is easy. Just look at the output generated by our activities over a period of time.

Becoming a Better Activity Chooser – What's important to do today?

Choosing activities effectively requires the ability to prioritize. Prioritizing involves the selection of those activities that are important to be initiated and completed in a given time frame. The highest priorities are activities that are Green (vital and not urgent) and Red (vital and urgent).

Since so many activities scream for our attention, it is helpful to use guidelines when making initial choices for the day. Suggested guidelines for establishing priorities include asking ourselves which activities:

- Give the greatest return for the time and energy invested?
- Are of greatest value to our organization's success?
- Preserve the well-being and performance of co-workers?
- Threaten the survival of our organization if not accomplished?
- Are Red (vital and urgent) and require an immediate response?
- Are Yellow (illusions) and should be rescheduled?

These guidelines can help set the most productive direction for the day. They can also help us overcome the natural human tendency to go for activities that are quick, fun, easy, and familiar; oftentimes Yellow and Gray events.

Becoming a Better Activity Arranger – How do I plan to accomplish my vital responsibilities?

Planning involves the ability to apply personally appropriate guidelines for arranging the order of activities selected. Personally appropriate means to arrange your activities in the order that makes you most productive. Your daily strategy should not be based upon some sort of planning formula suggested to you by some time management guru or outside consultant if it doesn't fit your personality.

Attempting to use the methods of someone else will force you to work in ways that are not as efficient and will almost guarantee ineffectiveness. Each of us performs at our best by working in ways that fit our own style and personality.

At the beginning of each day, I mentally visualize my most important activities on my way to work. When I arrive, I write them on a flip chart in my office space. I assign an employee name to each of the activities. These individuals comprise a daily team who work interactively among themselves as well as with me. We hold a team meeting at 8:30 a.m. to discuss each of the assignments, our interaction, and the timelines involved. Then, off we go to perform our assigned tasks. Now, the fun begins!

There are two primary ways of accomplishing tasks: *polychronic* and *monochronic*. A polychronic workstyle is one where several activities occur simultaneously. This style involves an unstructured, flexible mode of operation. A monochronic workstyle is one where essentially one activity occurs at a time, typically to completion. This style involves a structured, more defined mode of operation.

In our team operations, we have learned to use both styles. Some tasks are best performed using a polychronic approach and some using a monochromic approach. For example, in designing PowerPoint presentations, computer specialists, creative designers, and scriptwriters are simultaneously designing, changing, and improving all three tasks. On the other hand, when doing a sales presentation or a financial report, the best procedure is typically a logical, structured, and linear approach.

Arranging your important daily activities will inevitably involve working with a variety of co-workers, clients, and other individuals. This process can be productive and rewarding, or conflicting and stressful, depending on the variety of styles you experience and how skilled you are at adapting to them.

So what's your style—polychronic, monochronic, or a combination? Check one choice below for each numbered pair that represents your *dominant* style, even though you may do both on occasion.

Polychronic Style

1. _____ Relationship-oriented
2. _____ Do several activities simultaneously
3. _____ Socially expressive
4. _____ Open expression of feelings/emotions
5. _____ Focus on trust, sensitivity and communication
6. _____ People-oriented
7. _____ Informal
8. _____ Indirect
9. _____ Flexible
10. _____ Focused on the process

_____ **Total**

Monochronic Style

1. _____ Task-oriented
2. _____ Do activities in a linear manner
3. _____ Socially reserved
4. _____ Limited expression of feelings/emotions
5. _____ Focus on respect, strategy and systems
6. _____ Individually-oriented
7. _____ Formal
8. _____ Direct
9. _____ Fixed
10. _____ Focused on the goal

_____ **Total**

Understanding your own dominant style will influence how you plan, arrange, and execute your daily activities. Let's take a look at how these styles play out in workplace activities in the following section.

Allow Sufficient Time to Accomplish Planned Activities

Have you ever wondered why things usually take longer than you think they will? The major reason managers underestimate the time required is because they fail to make a distinction between polychronic and monochronic activities.

Monochronic activities are easiest to forecast because they are the most predictable. Monochronic time is based upon hours and minutes. For example: the meeting will last from 8-10 a.m.; your flight to Los Angeles will take one hour and twenty minutes once airborne; or, it takes ten minutes to hard-boil an egg.

Polychronic activities are less predictable and can rarely be measured by the clock. These activities involve people, creativity, analysis, intuition, spontaneity, and intangibles like introspection. How long does it take to create something, solve a problem, or resolve a conflict with somebody? We don't have the answers in advance. The key to scheduling polychronic activities is to allow extra time or arrange for certain types of meetings to be open-ended.

Medical doctors are involved in polychronic activity when dealing with patients. Perhaps this is why most are behind schedule. My doctor, however, constantly amazed me. He passed away recently. His name was Bob Poulsen. Whenever I showed up for an appointment he was always on schedule. He valued my time as much as his own. But here's what was always a mystery to me. After an exam, if he sensed I had a special concern on my mind, his formal countenance would change. He'd then sink into his office chair and talk as long as I wanted. He made me feel as though I was the most important person in the world. I never felt rushed.

I've often marveled at Dr. Poulsen's skill in managing his office. Clearly by nature, he was polychronic, but also operated his office efficiently and effectively. He had learned, through experience, that people are unpredictable and he had the wisdom to arrange his appointments accordingly. I learned a powerful principle from his example. Good managers have time for people. They have the skills to be both relationship and task oriented.

> **Good managers have time for people. They have the skills to be both relationship _and_ task-oriented.**

Here are some additional reasons why activities take longer than we think:

- Execution is almost always more difficult than our mental image of the activity
- Unexpected occurrences such as waiting for others
- Fatigue
- Interruptions from others
- Self-interruptions
- Overcoming personal inertia
- Not having the necessary tools on hand

When arranging activities for the day, if it's a polychronic activity, allow for extra time. A rule of thumb I personally use is an extra twenty percent more time than I think it will take.

Planning Your Day Made Easy

Some people have a real knack for planning. Many do not. If you are among those who struggle, I would like to introduce you to three coaches who will guide you in arranging your daily activities. They are: **necessity**, **practicality** and **efficiency**.

Necessity: These activities are locked in and not changeable. Examples include: child-care, customer appointments, meetings, maternity leave, emergencies, etc.

Practicality: Practicality involves arranging activities to be accomplished at the best time of day for the type of activity. Examples include: medical appointments, school activities, volunteerism, convenience-on-the-job, time off, vacations, personal energy cycles, etc.

Efficiency: The most effective utilization of resources is efficiency. Efficiency involves: mentoring and delegating, continuous improvement and quality, teamwork, etc.

The following questions will help you effectively assess necessity, practicality, and efficiency in arranging your activities for the day.

- Which activities are related to my goals?
- Which activities are locked into a time that cannot be changed?
- Am I allowing for personal centering/recovery time?
- How much buffer time should I allow between activities?
- Have I allocated time to respond to the unexpected?
- Does my schedule align my most difficult tasks with those times when my energy level is highest?
- What is the best time of day to do this type of activity?
- Have I set appointments with myself to ensure that the most vital activities are accomplished?
- Have I arranged my activities based upon the availability of others, if required?
- Is my plan efficient and practical?
- Can any of my planned activities be delegated?
- If my activities involve other people will they be available?
- Of my planned activities, which are absolutely necessary?

Maintaining touch with reality by determining the necessity, practicality, and efficiency of your activities allows you to arrange and forecast sufficient time to accomplish your planned activities.

Of course these guidelines can be applied effectively only through a personal commitment to plan a daily strategy each and every day. Setting an appointment with yourself to plan or arrange your day increases your likelihood of success.

Conversely, one of the biggest obstacles to a high-performance day and one of the biggest barriers to work-life balance is not taking the time to plan a daily strategy.

> *One of the biggest obstacles to a high-performance day and one of the biggest barriers to work-life quality and balance is not taking the time to plan a daily strategy.*

Just as it is advantageous to arrange your day based on the ways you do things best, personal management tools are also a matter of personal style and preference.

Scheduling and Planning – Electronic or Paper?

I was flying between Salt Lake City and Atlanta recently. Two executives were talking business. When the conversation changed to family it was suddenly time to share pictures. The man in the aisle seat simply took out his PDA (Personal Digital Assistant) and began showing photographs on his screen.

PDA computing is everywhere. We conduct surveys in some of our classes to see how many people come in with this type of computer. At management levels, in our classes, the average is about twenty-five percent. In some circles it is now fashionable to carry the latest PDA technology. Consequently, some are feeling peer pressure to trash the paper planner. But wait! Let's evaluate the pros and cons.

First, remember that all organizers, both paper and electronic, are designed to assist us in three general areas: *scheduling*, *journalizing*, and *information organizing*.

The *scheduler* consists of a monthly calendar and daily dated pages to plan your daily action list and to schedule appointments.

The *journal* is the place to record important details connected to dates and projects for future reference. A word of advice: If the dated journal page feature is missing there is a tendency to resort to note taking on random floating slips of paper. This practice tends to be riskier with a high probability of information loss.

The *information organizer* is where you keep key data at your fingertips so you can file and retrieve it quickly. This is the major benefit of a hand-held computer—it's a "bucket full" of information you can carry with you in an incredibly small space. The information organizer, as a paper tool, is usually organized in a tabbed index section.

So what's best for you? A hand-held computer only? A paper organizer only? Or does a blend of paper and electronic tools make sense? How do you decide?

My suggestion is to resist peer pressure long enough to evaluate what will really work for you. You will rarely be evaluated in your company by the tool you use. In most cases, your performance is of primary importance. With that in mind, let's think about how *you* function. Then we'll take a look at how the tools function and whether or not they facilitate or hinder your performance.

Before you make an investment of several hundred dollars, the following assessment will help you determine how compatible a hand-held electronic device is likely to be for your style. Put a check in front of the statement that best describes your situation.

	You are a *non-linear* person		You are a *linear* person
	Your job is mostly *stationary*		Your job requires you to be *mobile*
	You have a mostly *polychronic* workstyle		You have a mostly *monochronic* workstyle
	Your daily action list is dynamic—constantly *changing*		Your daily action list tends to be mostly static—*unchanging*
	You enjoy thinking and conceptualizing on *paper*		You enjoy thinking and conceptualizing on a *keyboard*

You are in meetings where you take a lot of notes	It is not necessary for you to take a lot of notes
You prefer the advantages of a *large* writing space	You prefer the advantages of *miniaturization* in a tool

If you scored higher in the left column it is likely that you would be most effective with a paper organizing tool or with a combination of paper and electronic. A significantly higher score in the right column indicates that you might work more effectively using a PDA, hand-held computer as your only instrument.

Personally, I prefer to use a combination of both. I'm finding that many individuals are also choosing to carry some sort of scheduler/information organizer in addition to their personal computer, even their laptops. This permits them to capitalize on the advantages of having a calendar, action list, and journal with them and conveniently accessible.

The key to successfully combining high-tech organizing with paper organizing is to minimize duplicating functions. For instance, I use the PC on my desk for database management and sales contacting. I use my laptop for presentations. I use my PDA computer to store information. And, because I'm a visual person, I carry a paper scheduler with my PDA computer to record appointments and all other calendar and journal items.

The president of a highly respected consulting firm uses a flip chart in the corner of his office to plan and prioritize his day. His future scheduled activities are posted on a paper calendar on his desk and he uses his PC for creative work. A leading attorney in Phoenix, Arizona, uses his Palm™ V exclusively as his time management tool and uses virtually no paper.

Of course you'll need to experiment to determine ultimately what works for you but there is one thing you can count on—

Electronic tools _and_ paper tools are both here to stay.

Focusing on Activities

In the first paragraph of this chapter we talked about the essential principle—the skill that allows you to get the very best return on your investment of time and personal resources. In fact, everything I've recommended so far has been aimed at helping you achieve this skill. It is the skill of *concentration of power.* It is the overarching principle in effective self-management. It is a survival skill to be used in an environment of distractions, interruptions, change, and uncertainty.

Focusing involves the ability to concentrate your undivided attention, your mental energy, on the achievement of your planned, and even your unplanned activities. This is accomplished by avoiding, or at least minimizing, distractions or intrusions except those that are truly urgent. Suggestions for focusing based on the experiences of workplace personnel fall into two categories: 1) Setting the Environment and, 2) Avoiding Distractions.

Setting the Environment

- ✓ Turn off the telephone, radio, or other disturbances, when focusing is required
- ✓ Make sure you have all the tools you need before you start
- ✓ Unclutter your desk or work space and remove unrelated items
- ✓ Close your door or create a private place where appropriate or necessary

Avoiding Distractions

- ✓ Where appropriate, be direct and clear that you do not want to be interrupted
- ✓ Adopt an attitude of self-responsibility for getting things done
- ✓ Use an electronic or paper management tool to track events and free your mind
- ✓ When everyone is clear about your focusing time they will learn to adapt accordingly

Utilize the Principle of Accessibility

Simple concepts can be powerful. When used they are often the difference between success and failure. One of the most powerful yet underutilized concepts in the field of achievement is the principle of accessibility.

The earliest formal writing we can find on the subject is by Charles R. Hobbs, Ph.D., in his doctoral thesis written while attending Columbia University. Dr. Hobbs clarifies the essence of this idea in these words, "If you would induct yourself into a skill, an element of knowledge, or a goal, make that skill, knowledge, or goal directly, continuously, and meaningfully accessible to yourself."

Simply stated, if you desire to succeed in achieving a goal or acquiring a new skill, keep it visible. Keep the goal constantly accessible as a reminder and motivator.

> *If you desire to succeed in achieving a goal or acquiring a new skill, keep it visible as a reminder and a motivator.*

Actually, it was a high school senior who helped me appreciate this idea more fully through her personal application of the principle of accessibility. After graduation from high school several years ago, Mary wanted to reward herself with a trip to Europe, but she didn't have the money. At that time, travel to Europe wasn't as accessible as it is today! Using the principle of accessibility she bought a large map of the world and taped it on her bedroom wall.

When she had enough money to fly from Los Angeles to Denver she drew a line on the map between those two cities. Soon the line was halfway across the country then all the way to the east coast. Excitement for Mary built as her ever-growing line grew to halfway across the Atlantic Ocean and finally to Paris. Her dream became a reality.

Every morning and every evening that map was in her face as a constant reminder and motivator. It works! Seldom do I personally achieve my goals without implementing the principle of accessibility. This year I've decided to take a *virtual* 750-mile walk from Salt Lake City to San Francisco. A map is on my office wall, just as Mary taught me. I walk the same loop in my condominium community and surrounding neighborhood, or hike the same trails in the nearby canyons every week. I add my miles and mark my map accordingly. As my line gets farther across the map each week, I visualize my goal being achieved.

As part of accessibility I've told my neighbors what I'm doing. As they drive by in their cars they cheer me on! Some times they stop and ask, "Where are you now?" I shout out, "Reno!" Enrolling friends to assist you with keeping your goal accessible can also be part of the technique.

To further secure accessibility of my virtual walk to San Francisco, I've promised myself a reward. My wife and I are going to fly to San Francisco and meet my virtual self at the completion of that 750-mile walk. We will then dine in a favorite restaurant in the Bay Area. I visualize that experience at least weekly.

So what do you hope to achieve this year? How is your focus? Are you leveraging the power of accessibility? What about goals you had hoped to achieve in the past but did not? Was accessibility missing? Accessible means "capable of being reached." There is hardly anything that provides more satisfaction than stretching for and reaching a goal. At the beginning of each new year, I make a list of the major things I want to accomplish for the coming year. I post them in some visible place in my office. I also write them on the back of a business card and read them at least once a week. The question I always ask is, "Are my activities in alignment with my written goals?" Where the answer is "No," I make the appropriate adjustments.

Practice the principle of accessibility to assist you in staying focused over periods of time.

Accomplish Your Plans Efficiently and Effectively

In the process of accomplishing activities that are vital, urgent activities will appear. Clearly, in the new environment, we must be flexible. But being flexible does not mean we throw caution to the wind and forget about being efficient and effective. Efficiency refers to maximizing the use of resources such as time, money, people, etc. Effectiveness refers to using the best procedure or method to arrive at, or exceed, the desired outcome.

> *Efficiency refers to maximizing the use of resources, such as time, money, people, etc. Effectiveness refers to using the best procedure or method to arrive at, or exceed, the desired outcome.*

It is prudent to expect the unexpected each day. When an unexpected activity occurs requiring your attention, the most efficient and effective action you can take is to categorize it as either vital or not vital. Once you've made that determination, select the best options for addressing it. Typical examples of unexpected activities follow. With the traffic light metaphor in mind (page 83), making fast, quick decisions about how to deal with these and others should be less daunting. What would you do or how would you respond to the following urgent situations?

Situation One

You have put off dealing with an ongoing problem with a co-worker but now he/she is going to bring the conflict to your boss for resolution.

Situation Two

During the course of a busy day, a sales representative drops by to inform you of the latest product-offering key to your operation. He/she says, "It will only take a couple of minutes." But you know from previous experience it will be at least one hour.

Situation Three

One hour before a critical sales presentation to a key customer you get a call that your child has had a minor accident at school and was taken to the local hospital.

Situation Four

During the course of a busy day, when you have a series of critical appointments, a personal friend calls to inform you that his wife has just asked for a divorce. He's emotionally shaken and asks if he can talk with you ASAP. Some of your appointments with high-level executives have been arranged for several months.

In our seminars, most participants treat situation two as a Yellow activity and they are divided on situations one, three, and four. What about you? The point is, as the unexpected occurs during the day, we need to be able to make *quick* and *appropriate* decisions about the many events confronting us. We should not be sidetracked by some interruptions we can and should reschedule. Many people don't do this. Many of us handle interruptions in the order they occur, not the order of their priority.

Do you want more quality and balance during your day? Remember you have the power to reschedule some interruptions. That way you can handle them in the order of priority, not in the order they occur.

Afterword

More than Footprints on the Moon – What Legacy Will You Leave Behind?

"Some men see things as they are and say 'why?'
I see things as they never were, and ask 'why not?'"

George Bernard Shaw

That night in Houston, Texas, when I had dinner with Apollo 15 Astronaut Jim Irwin, he told me a secret. He said, "Nobody knows this, but when I was on the moon I had with me a piece of paper on which I'd written the names of my family members. There, in a space moment, I used it to build a monument to my family. I left that paper and my footprints on the moon. Do you realize that because the moon has no atmosphere, that monument and my footprints will be there for a least a million years?"

Whenever I look up at the moon I think about Jim's family. I can't help but believe they are reminded every time they look into the heavens that their dad built a monument to them, reminding them to soar. What a legacy!

What kind of legacy will you leave on Spaceship Earth for those you love? Jim Irwin left footprints on the moon. Each of us is similar to Jim. Figuratively, we all leave footprints in the sands of time. We do this with every activity we perform. Will you be remembered by those who matter most to you as a person who was 100% responsible and 100% accountable for your life? Will they remember that you lived every moment with all your heart? Or will you be remembered for the victim role you played, completely missing your full potential for a quality life?

What script will you choose to write and live? It's up to you. It really is your choice. You can choose to live, love, earn, and serve in a way that fills your life with more contentment, more excitement, more happiness, more passion, more quality, and consequently, more satisfaction. You really can leave behind a legacy of integrity and inspiration.

My sincerest best wishes for you as you rewrite and live the rest of *your* life story!

Quick Reference Vocabulary Words

Activity: an event that you initiate—both consciously and unconsciously.

Event: anything that happens, from catastrophic events that no one person has control over to something as simple as a mosquito landing on your arm.

Effective: using the best procedure or method in achieving a desired outcome.

Efficient: maximizing resources, (time, money, assets, people, etc.) in achieving a desired outcome.

Innermost values: those that come from within you, beyond those superficially defined by society. They are enduring over time, transcending recognition, advancement, and reward.

Personal responsibility: the willingness to be the principal source of what happens in your life.

Personal accountability: the willingness to own the results that occur in your life.

Personal empowerment: an internal motivation to perform at or above an established level of expectation.

Priority: a valued activity.

Urgency: critical, life threatening, serious, severe, acute; a situation or condition that requires immediate action.

Vital: very important, fundamental, essential, imperative, or central.

Work-life integration: the *alternate* execution of work and personal life activities in a manner that permits us to fully experience both.

Work-life contamination: the *simultaneous* execution of work and personal life activities in a manner that prevents us from fully experiencing both.

About the Authors

William A. Guillory, Ph.D. is the CEO and founder of Innovations Consulting International, Inc. He has presented more than 4,000 seminars throughout corporate America, Europe, Asia Pacific, Mexico, and Canada. He has facilitated seminars for over 300 corporations, including the senior management of American Airlines, Avon Products, Inc., Eastman Kodak Company, Electronic Data Systems, Lockheed Martin Corporation, Sandia National Laboratories, Rohm and Haas Company, Texas Instruments, Sempra Energy, DaimlerChrysler, Kellogg Corporation, and many other Fortune 500 corporations.

Dr. Guillory is an authority on diversity, empowerment, leadership, creativity, and work-life quality and balance. He is a widely requested and popular conference and keynote speaker on these subjects as well as spirituality in the workplace. He is the author of four books on personal transformation, *"Realizations,"* *"It's All an Illusion," "Destined to Succeed,"* and *"The Guides,"* and is the co-author of the management book titled "EMPOWERMENT *For High Performing Organizations."* His most recent book is "The Living Organization – *Spirituality in the Workplace."*

Prior to establishing Innovations, Dr. Guillory was a physical chemist of international renown. His distinguished awards and appointments include an Alfred P. Sloan Fellowship, an Alexander von Humboldt appointment at the University of Frankfurt, a Ralph Metcalf Chair at Marquette University, and the Chancellor's Distinguished Lectureship at the University of California at Berkeley. Dr. Guillory founded Innovations in 1985 following a period of intense personal growth which led to a career change to individual and organization transformation.

Warren "Trapper" Woods, CSP is president and CEO of Cannonwood. With a career that spans more than thirty-five years, Trapper Woods, also known as FatherTime™, is an executive leader, corporate consultant, company president, business owner, and internationally acclaimed speaker. He has traveled more than 2 million miles influencing tens of thousands of people in over 350 corporations throughout the United States, Canada, the United Kingdom, and the Caribbean. Trapper is a well-known authority in the field of personal effectiveness and has served as consultant to some of the world's most influential time management companies. Trapper is described as the catalyst that inspires individuals and organizations to increase their capacity to perform through confident, effective self-management skills. His engaging style is the result of his fundamental belief in the goodness inherent within each person and the value of diversity.

Innovations International, Inc.

Innovations International, Inc.

Innovations is a global human resource development corporation specializing in personal and organizational transformation. We exist to assist organizations in achieving their business performance goals while maintaining their personal and collective well-being.

Our specializations in consulting include:

- Diversity
- Empowerment
- Leadership
- Creativity and Innovation
- Quantum-Thinking
- Work-Life Quality and Balance
- Spirituality in the Workplace

These specializations include comprehensive programs involving consulting, seminars, audits and assessments, coaching, strategic planning, and interactive multimedia learning.

Our multimedia and online series in Diversity and High Performance feature CD-ROM interactive processes including video presentations and scenarios, question and answer discussions, interactive case studies, and self-management skills.

For information regarding Innovations' programs, telephone, write, fax, Email, or visit our web page:

Innovations International, Inc.
310 East 4500 South, Suite 420
Salt Lake City, UT 84107 USA
Tel: (801) 268-3313
Fax: (801) 268-3422
Email: **innovationsintl@qwest.net**
Web site: **www.innovint.com**

Cannonwood

Cannonwood is a training organization specializing in helping individuals increase effectiveness, adapt to a changing business environment, and balance their lives. Our method of delivery is through corporate, public, web-based, and self-paced training programs.

Cannonwood is Day-Timer®'s Training Partner in presenting the world-renowned TimePower®, developed by Charles R. Hobbs, Ph.D. In addition to TimePower®, we offer business seminars in the following areas:

- Diversity
- Empowerment
- Customer Service
- Leadership

For information regarding Cannonwood's programs, telephone, write, Email, or visit our web page:

Cannonwood
3945 South Wasatch Blvd.
Salt Lake City, Utah 84124
Tel: (888) 972-0800
Email: **trapperwoods@cannonwood.com**
Website: **www.cannonwood.com**